Patrick Duigenan

Lachrymæ academicæ

Or the Present Deplorable State of the College of the Holy and Undivided Trinity, of

Queen Elizabeth, near Dublin

Patrick Duigenan

Lachrymæ academicæ
Or the Present Deplorable State of the College of the Holy and Undivided Trinity, of Queen Elizabeth, near Dublin

ISBN/EAN: 9783337280857

Printed in Europe, USA, Canada, Australia, Japan

Cover: Foto ©Suzi / pixelio.de

More available books at **www.hansebooks.com**

LACHRYMÆ ACADEMICÆ;

OR, THE

PRESENT DEPLORABLE STATE

OF THE

COLLEGE

OF THE

HOLY AND UNDIVIDED TRINITY,
OF QUEEN ELIZABETH, NEAR DUBLIN.

MOST HUMBLY DEDICATED

TO HIS MAJESTY.

BY

PATRICK DUIGENAN, L. L. D.

Royal Profeſſor of Feudal and Engliſh Law, in the Univerſity of Dublin:
Late one of the Fellows, and Member of the Board, of the ſaid College.

——— QUÆQUE IPSE MISERRIMA VIDI,
ET QUORUM PARS MAGNA FUI.———
VIRGIL ÆNEID.

DUBLIN:

Printed for the AUTHOR, and ſold by all the BOOKSELLERS.
M,DCC,LXXVII.

TO THE

K   I   N   G's

MOST EXCELLENT MAJESTY:

MOST GRACIOUS SOVEREIGN,

FILLED with the ideas of your Majesty's piety, wisdom, justice and benevolence, the author of the following treatise, presumes to lay it at your feet: indebted to the princely munificence of your Majesty, and your royal predecessors, for his present rank in life; and educated, from his earliest youth, in the principles of loyalty to the crown, and attachment to the constitution of his country, in church and state, he ventures to approach your Majesty, as the advocate of religion, morality, and learning: to whom

DEDICATION.

can they fly for protection and relief, with so much propriety as to
your Majesty, who is the true father
of your people, the ornament of hu-
manity, the perfect model of every
christian virtue, and the munificent
patron of the arts and sciences. Relying on your Majesty's equity, wisdom and generosity, their cause is
most humbly submitted to your Majesty's consideration, by

YOUR MAJESTY'S,

MOST HUMBLE,

MOST DUTIFUL,

MOST FAITHFUL

Chancery-lane,   SUBJECT AND SERVANT,
Dublin, July 6, 1777.

PATRICK DUIGENAN.

PREFACE.

As the promotion of the Right Hon. John Hely Hutchinſon, one of his Majeſty's *Privy Council,* in Ireland, *Honorary Doctor of Laws,* and a *practiſing* Barriſter, to the place of Provoſt of Trinity College, Dublin, has ſtruck people in general, with more amazement, and has been already, and is ſtill likely to be, attended with more ruinous conſequences, as well to that College, as to the whole kingdom of Ireland, than any one ſtep which has been taken by the ſucceſſive governors of that kingdom, ſince the reign of Queen Elizabeth; I ſhall, in the following ſheets, firſt explain the motives which induced Earl Harcourt, Vice-roy of Ireland, to recommend Mr. Hutchinſon to his Majeſty, as a proper perſon to ſucceed the late Provoſt : in the next place, I ſhall diſpaſſionately inquire, whether he is capable of performing the duties of his ſtation ; and laſtly, I ſhall faithfully ſtate to the publick,

PREFACE.

lick, in a detail of incontrovertible facts, the manner in which he thinks fit to govern the College. I am indebted to the College of Dublin for my education, and my prefent employment; I was a member of it for twenty three years and upwards, and one of its Fellows for fifteen years; my moft valuable friends are at prefent Fellows of it, but, from the rigour of it's ftatutes, deprived even of the poor confolation of complaint for the injuries and infults already heaped upon them, and which they daily fuffer. I cannot therefore, fit an unconcerned fpectator of its mifery and ruin : but if none of thefe motives had exifted to incite me to my prefent undertaking, yet my regard for the intereft of learning and religion, would fufficiently ftimulate me to make an effort, however weak, to prevent their total extirpation from this realm, in which they were fo happily planted by the renowned Elizabeth. The conduct of Mr. Hutchinfon to me, whilft I remained a Fellow, will appear, in the following fheets, candidly related : But left it fhould be afferted, or infinuated by him or his friends (if any friends he has) that my private animofity againft him, on account of

his

his infolent and injurious behaviour to me
(and not the motives which I have juft mentioned) have influenced me to this publication, I think it neceffary to declare, that I never entertained even the thought of expreff-
ing my private refentment by a pen, and that
I never would have inferted, in the following
fheets, one line concerning any tranfaction
which has paffed between Mr. Hutchinfon
and me, but from the confideration that
thefe infults and injuries were heaped upon
me, as a Fellow of the College, in the exercife of my duty, and for my faithful difcharge
of it : And that he never would have ventured to infult me, had I not been a Fellow,
and, as it were, bound hand and foot, by
the chains of the ftatutes ; fo that my ftation, not I, was infulted ; and as his outrageous behaviour, to the members of the
College, is one of its many grievances, and
naturally falls under that part of my fubject
which relates to his conduct in the government of it, it is abfolutely neceffary that I
fhould mention his conduct to me, as well as
to the other members. In the performance of
this tafk, nothing whatfoever fhall induce
me to deviate, in the fmalleft degree, from
the

the truth : I fhall fet forth fuch facts only, refpecting his conduct in the College, as I can prove before the venerable Vifitors (when their graces fhall think proper to give me an opportunity of doing fo) by a number of the moft refpectable witneffes : as one confiderable part of my defign in the following publication, is to roufe up the publick to call for, and the Vifitors to commence, a ftatutable examination into the conduct of Mr. Hutchinfon, before the ruin of this unfortunate feminary fhall be completed, I will take care not to amufe either the Publick or their graces with ill-founded or trifling charges. I think I am in full poffeffion of fuch Facts, as muft convince every thinking perfon, that, if he is fuffered to remain unpunifhed and uncontrolled at the head of the College, for fo fhort a term as five years from hence, the College will no longer exift ; that is, the building may remain in its prefent condition : but religion, morality and literature (for the promotion of all which it was founded) will be exiled from its walls; its revenues will be, for the greater part, wafted and deftroyed by himfelf, his children, his fervants, his dependants
and

his tools ; and the reft appropriated to the
fupport of a pack of indigent, illiterate
wretches, who will engage to vote at elections for fuch perfons as he fhall think fit to
nominate reprefentatives in parliament for
the College, and to infult fuch members of
the Univerfity and College, as he fhall think
fit to halloo them at ; care will be taken to
provide fucceffors to this gang, with fimilar
qualifications ; and thus, in the language of
our bleffed Saviour, the College, from being
the *houfe of prayer*, will become a *den of
thieves*.

LACHRYMÆ ACADEMICÆ,

OR

THE PRESENT DEPLORABLE STATE

OF THE

COLLEGE, &c.

THE College of the holy and undivided Trinity, of queen Elizabeth, near Dublin, is the only feminary of learning in the kingdom of Ireland, and the mother of the University of Dublin. The fagacious queen, whofe name honours the title of this College, obferving that ignorance had over-fpread the face of her realm of Ireland, and knowing ignorance to be the parent of fuperftition and bigotry, which were craftily made ufe of, by her foreign and domeftick enemies, to foment difcontents and excite rebellions amongft her

B   fubjects

subjects there, thought the most effectual method to establish peace, to diffuse the true light of the gospel, and consequently to banish superstition, and its pernicious attendants, was, to encourage learning, and the culture of the sciences in that kingdom, and for that purpose she was pleased to found this College, and to endow it with considerable estates in land, *and also a yearly pension out of her exchequer.* It flourished and increased in her auspicious reign, and in the reigns of her successors (by the favour of the crown and parliament, and the generosity of private Benefactors) to such a degree, that whether we consider the extent and beauty of its buildings, the number of its students, the learning of its Fellows and other members, the value of its estates, foundations, and endowments for the encouragement of every kind of literature, or the wisdom of its institutions, it certainly had no equal in Europe as a single college, and was superior to most Universities, at the time Mr. Hutchinson was promoted to the government of it. As this portentous promotion is the malady,

which

which not only threatens, but enfures, the
fpeedy diffolution of this glorious eftablifhment, if effectual remedies are not in time
applied, and as the beft method of finding
out a remedy, is to inveftigate the nature, and
attain a true knowledge of the diforder ; I
fhall lay before the Publick the caufes, nature,
extent and progrefs of the difeafe, and
afterwards point out effectual remedies for it,
and the proper way of procuring them.

In the reign of king Charles the firft, the
lord deputy Wentworth, afterwards the famous and unfortunate earl of Strafford, and
the no lefs famous and unfortunate William
Laud, Archbifhop of Canterbury, thought
fit, for fome reafons not neceffary to be recited here, to new model the College of Dublin, and the ftatutes thereof, and prevailed on
the then Provoft and Fellows to furrender the
old Charter of queen Elizabeth into the
hands of the Crown. A new charter and
body of ftatutes, compiled by archbifhop
Laud, were granted to the College ; which
contained almoft an entire new code of laws

B 2   for

for the government of it. The changes
made by the new charter and ftatutes, as far
as they relate to my prefent fubject, I fhall
briefly mention. By the charter of queen
Elizabeth, the Fellows of the College had
the power of electing a Provoft, on a vacancy : By the charter of Charles, the power
of nominating a Provoft is referved to the
crown. By the former charter, the power
of electing Fellows and Scholars, on vacancies, was given to the Provoft and Fellows:
By the latter charter and ftatutes, this power is, in effect, lodged in the Provoft alone:
for the candidates, both for Fellowfhips and
Scholarfhips, are all obliged to undergo a fevere and critical examination, previous to
the election, and tho' there is a formal
election held, and the electors (who are the
Provoft and Senior Fellows) are folemnly
fworn to act with impartiality, yet it is provided by thefe new ftatutes, that the Provoft muft always be one of the voters for
the fuccefsful Candidate, and that if a
majority of the Senior Fellows fhould
not vote for fuch candidate as the Provoft
votes

votes for, after two fcrutinies, the candidate whom he thinks fit to nominate fhall be confidered as elected, tho' he fhould not have one vote, except the Provoft's. Thus the Provoft has it in his power to nominate all the fellows and fcholars. An immoderate power is alfo lodged in the Provoft in many other things by thefe new ftatutes; particularly a power of putting a negative on any refolution whatfoever of the board, compofed of the feven fenior fellows, which can not, when he is prefent, be of any force without his confent: this, in a great meafure, throws into his hands the whole diftribution of academick emoluments and rewards, which in this college are very confiderable; for tho' he cannot actually difpofe of them without the confent of the board, yet he can prevent their being conferred on any perfons, but fuch as he approves of. In regard to collegiate punifhments, thefe new ftatutes have armed the Provoft with a ftill greater and more unreafonable power: for in refpect to the infliction of thefe, he has not only the fame negative power, as in the

conferring

conferring of rewards, so that he may screen
all such offenders as he pleases from punishment, but he is authorized to call before
him any member of the College, whom he
may think fit to accuse, or cause to be accused, of any of those crimes, which are called
in the statutes *Majora Crimina*, or greater
crimes, and expel him, if he confesses the
crime, or is convicted of it by sufficient wit-
nesses; and, as he is in this case the sole
judge, he may decree, that any person
testifying any thing whatsoever is a sufficient witness, to prove the crime to be
committed; and he may also try and judge
any member of the College, in his own
private apartment, without any witness
whatsoever, and then he has only to declare, that the accused person confessed the
crime, which he thought fit to lay to his
charge, or was convicted of it, and call upon
the two Deans, the senior and junior, to
put his sentence in execution; for they are
only his ministers, and not his affessors, in
this case. What makes this power still
more intolerable is, that in the enumeration

of

of the *Majora Crimina,* or greater crimes, in the ſtatutes, there are certain general expreſ-ſions made uſe of, within the vague ſignifi-cations of which he may include any crime, or even an innocent action; and thus he may drag to his ſole tribunal the cognizance of any offence whatſoever, committed by a member of the College, or may conſtrue ac-tions, in themſelves innocent, into *Majora Crimina, et Miſera eſt Servitus ubi Lex eſt vaga et Incognita.* Another circumſtance which makes this ſole power of the Provoſt, regarding the *Majora Crimina* to appear as abſurd as it is unjuſt, is, that with reſpect to what are called *Minora Crimina,* or leſſer crimes, by the ſtatutes, tho' he can by his negative power ſcreen any offender from puniſhment, yet he cannot inflict any pun-iſhment for a *Minus Crimen* without the conſent of the majority of the board. Thus theſe new ſtatutes have armed the Provoſt with a deſpotick power, in all things regard-ing the greater crimes, and a limited one, with reſpect to the leſſer; as if the preven-tion and ſuppreſſion of leſſer evils required

the

the joint wifdoms of the whole board, but of greater, the wifdom of the eighth part of that board only, which confifts of the Provoft and feven fenior Fellows. In refpect to the College eftate and the management of it, by the new ftatutes, no leafe whatfoever can be made of any part of it, without the confent and approbation of the Provoft : this throws into his hands almoft the whole management of the property of the College. Thus by the new charter and ftatutes the Provoft is invefted with the fole power of creating all the members of the College; of difpofing of, and managing, in a great meafure, the whole revenues of it ; and of rewarding and punifhing, even with expulfion, according to his pleafure: fo that he can create, elevate, deprefs, and annihilate the whole body at his will. 'Tis true indeed, (and happily for the College it is fo) that this domination is but *Imperium fub Imperio*; for the Provoft is nominated by the crown, and in many particulars fubject to the power of it, particularly if he is unfit for the employment; and incapable of performing the duties of it, as I fhall fhew

in

in the progrefs of this work : he is alfo fubject to the *control* of the vifitors, who, by
the ftatutes, are the Chancellor of the Univerfity, or, in his abfence, the Vice-Chancellor, and the Archbifhop of Dublin for
the time being. They, as vifitors, are empowered, by the common law of the realm, to
repair to the College, at any time when a
grievance is complained of, to examine into
the nature of the complaint, afford fuch relief to the complainant as the cafe requires,
and expel any member of the College, even
the Provoft himfelf, if they difcover any offence to have been committed by him worthy of fuch a punifhment. This * power is
incident to their vifitatorial office. They are
alfo authorized, adjured, and entreated, in
the moft folemn manner, by the ftatutes, to
repair to the College once in every period of
three years, and inquire minutely into the
ftate of the College, and the government
thereof; to punifh all crimes and tranfgreffions, according to their quality and de-
fert,

* See Shower's Parliamentary Cafes, and Lord Raymond's
Reports; Cafe of Philips and Bury.

fert, and to proceed even to the expulfion of the Provoft himfelf, if they fhall fee occafion.

Thus far it was neceffary for me to explain the origin and conftitution of this College to the Publick, to enable them to form ideas of its prefent miferable and ruinous ftate, and to qualify them for underftanding the neceffity of an immediate application of the ftatutable remedies to prevent its diffolution. I fhall now, in purfuance of my original plan, proceed to lay before the Publick the caufes which led to Mr. Hutchinfon's promotion to the place of Provoft.

Francis Andrews, L. L. D. the late Provoft, after being afflicted for two years with a languifhing diforder, died fomewhat fuddenly in England, in June 1774. As the promotion of this gentleman, who was a layman, to the Provoftfhip, gave fome offence and difguft to the nation, and as it cannot be denied, that it, in fome meafure, fmoothed the way for the promotion of the prefent Provoft, it will be neceffary for me to ftate the pretenfions of Dr. Andrews to

the

the Provoſtſhip, in order to ſhew, however his promotion to that office may have been miſrepreſented, and made uſe of to induce his Majeſty to elevate the preſent Provoſt to that ſtation, that the qualifications and pre-tenſions of the two men were widely differ-ent : or, to ſpeak with propriety, that Dr. Andrews had great qualifications for, and pretenſions to, the office of Provoſt ; and Mr. Hutchinſon none whatſoever. Dr. Andrews, before he was appointed Pro-voſt, had been, for fifteen years and upwards, one of the Fellows of the College, and, for ſome part of that time, a ſenior Fellow. He was competently ſkilled in all the ſcien-tifick parts of learning, and eminently in polite literature : ſo that, as a ſenior Fellow and a ſcholar, he was equally qualified for, and entitled to, the place of Provoſt, with any other member of the College. It is true he was a layman and a doctor of law ; and the ſtatutes require that the Provoſt ſhould be a Clerick, and a doctor or batchelor in di-vinity : but the crown having reſerved to it-ſelf, by the new charter, a power of changing, altering,

altering, and difpenfing with the ftatutes, thought proper to difpenfe with this part of the ftatutes in favour of Dr. Andrews. He was a man of gentlemanly education and behaviour, and, tho' naturally of a warm temper, he took care never to let his warmth hurry him into indecency, much lefs outrage. He governed the College for fixteen years with great reputation, and, except in one inftance, never exerted the exorbitant power vefted in the Provoft, to the oppreffion of any member of the College; and, in this one inftance too, he had received much provocation from the petulance and obftinacy of the objeſt of his refentment. At the time of this gentleman's death, the Earl of Harcourt was Lord Lieutenant of Ireland; and whether it was, that his lordfhip (as fome people reported) was a man, whofe genius did not enable or incline him to conduſt bufinefs; or whether he thought that the fureft and moft expeditious method of effeſting the bufinefs of government was to make ufe of means, *in which it would be more honourable for him to have any other perfon rather than himfelf*

appear

appear the agent; or from what other motive
it happened, I cannot tell : but certain it is,
that he delegated his whole authority and
power to his fecretary, a man called Blacquiere. Who he was, fave that he had been
an officer of dragoons, no man could with
certainty tell : his origin, like the fource of
the Nile, was only gueffed at; but it was eafily perceived, that he was vain, infolent,
avaricious, ignorant and illiterate. In fome
meafure to remedy the contempt, which infolence, joined to low birth and education,
generally meets, and to give fome importance to this fecretary, his patron
caufed him to be created a Knight of the
Bath. This was the man, who, during the
whole period of Earl Harcourt's government,
diftributed all the preferments of the kingdom ; and he diftributed them, civil, military and ecclefiaftical, exactly according
to the value, at which he eftimated the
intereft or fervice in Parliament of the
perfons he conferred them on, or their
ability to ferve himfelf, without any regard
whatfoever to propriety, or even common
decency,

decency, in the appointments; for it was a
settled maxim with him, the result as well
of his avarice as ignorance, that any man
was sufficiently qualified to execute all manner of employments; and so fantastick were
the promotions he made, that the Lord
Lieutenant's levee became a complete maf-
querade. 'Tis true some men of merit procured employments from him, for which
they were well qualified; but they were very few, and owed their preferments to an interest which he was afraid to offend, or to any
thing, rather than merit or qualifications
for their places: for Blacquiere seemed to
have a fixed averfion from promoting any
perfon to an office, the duty of which he
was qualified to perform.. In fhort, he was
one of thofe perfons whom Juvenal defcribes.

" Quales ex humili magna ad faftigia rerum
" Extollit, quoties voluit fortuna jocari."

Unfortunately for the College, at the
time of Dr. Andrews's death, the place of
Solicitor-general was vacant, or rather was
immediately

immediately to be vacated, on the promotion of the then Solicitor-general to the bench in the Common Pleas, where there was a vacancy. The place of Solicitor was fought for by two gentlemen, either of which the Secretary did not choofe to difoblige, or rather wifhed to oblige one, and was afraid, for fome weighty reafons, to difoblige the other. In this dilemma, he received with joy the news of a vacancy in the College, as it gave him an opportunity of efcaping from his difficulty, and alfo fecuring to himfelf a lucrative place, by the promotion of Mr. Hutchinfon to the Provoftfhip. This gentleman, between whofe character and qualities, and thofe of Blacquiere, there is a great fimilarity, is a perfon unconfcionable in his demands on government. No poft or employment, of any kind or nature whatfoever, has become vacant, fince he was firft taken into the fervice of adminiftration, which he has not afked, either for himfelf or his dependants. So ridiculous are his vanity and ignorance, that he thinks himfelf perfectly capable of performing the duties of the different pofts of

Lord

Lord Chancellor, General, Bifhop, and of all other employments at the fame time; and fo unbounded his avarice and impudence, that he would afk for every employment and office in the gift of the Crown, in one breath, if they were vacant; and affect to think himfelf ill treated, and complain bitterly, if he was refufed. This temper of folicitation, or more properly efflagitation, amongft his other qualifications, had greatly conduced to procure for him and his children fome honourable and lucrative employments and reverfions, before his appointment to the Provoftfhip. He was himfelf Alnager of Ireland, which he farmed out at the clear yearly rent of £800. and procured an additional falary to be annexed to this employment, whilft it fhould remain in his poffeffion, of £1000 per annum, &c. He was alfo his Majefty's Prime Serjeant at Law, worth £1000 per ann. then was, and ftill is a Privy Counfellor, and had, and yet retains, the reverfion of the place of principal Secretary of State, worth £1800 per ann. His eldeft fon has the reverfion of the place of fecond

Remembrancer

Remembrancer of the Exchequer, worth £800 per ann. and has lately been appointed one of the Commiffioners of accounts, worth £500 per ann. His fecond fon has a troop of dragoons, or a company of foot, and all his relations and dependants, even fo low down as his Butler, have places and employments of fome kind or other, under or by government. It may be, perhaps, here afked, by thofe who are ftrangers to this kingdom (for here he is fufficiently known) who this perfon is, and what are his qualifications, who appears to have been fo well provided for by government? To which it may be anfwered, with truth, that he is a perfon who was bred to the profeffion of the law; that during the Lieutenancy of the Duke of Bedford, in this kingdom, he bought a feat in parliament, for a borough; that immediately after taking his feat in the houfe of commons, having the advantages of ftrong lungs, confummate affurance, a copious flow of words, and a fufficiently graceful delivery, he commenced a moft violent and obftreperous patriot. Luckily, in refpect to his own advancement, he had a very confined underftanding, fo that he could thun-

C

der

der forth nonfenfe for whole days together, with the moft furious diftortions of his vifage and the reft of his body, without being at all fenfible of the abfurdity and inanity of his own declamations : the fhame which muft be the companion of fuch a fenfation, even in his breaft, would have fealed up his mouth, and robbed him of all powers of utterance: yet the femblance of an orator I admit he is, and I have been amazed at obferving, " *How fluent nonfenfe trickled from his " tongue.*"

Thefe qualifications recommended him to government ; after patriotizing for a feffion or two in the houfe of commons, he was taken into the fervice of adminiftration, who have dearly enough purchafed the ufe of his talents, fuch as they are. This gentleman, who was conftantly on the watch for all places, which were either vacant, or likely to be fo, obferving the declining ftate of health of the late Provoft, had caft a wiftful eye on the Provoftfhip, for near a year before the vacancy happened ; and, as he is not deftitute of that fpecies of low cunning, practifed by mountebanks, and fuch kind of people, he thought his pretending to the
knowledge

knowledge of fome branches of learning
would conduce much to the completion of
his wifhes : not that he was at all fearful of
his friend Blacquiere's making any objection
againft his advancement to the Provoftfhip,
on the fcore of his being entirely illiterate,
and unqualified for the place, even if that
gentleman had been capable of judging whether he was fo, or not; but, becaufe the
College of Dublin, being the only feminary
of learning in Ireland, and the prefervation
or ruin of it being a matter of real national
importance, he was apprehenfive, that his
promotion, to the government of it, would be
a caufe of great popular clamour, unlefs he
took pains to perfuade people, that he was,
in fome meafure, qualified for the poft.
With this view, for near a year before the
death of Dr. Andrews, during his attendance at the Bar, he took frequent opportunities of difcourfing with the Barrifters about
the clafficks; telling them, that he always
relaxed from the toils of his profeffion, by
reading fome of the moft eminent Greek authors : but he never ventured to wade farther,
in any converfation about the clafficks, than
to repeat their names, and tell how often

he

he had read them : he, now and then, too,
threw out a little fhred of criticifm, or fcrap
of philofophy, collected from magazines,
reviews, and annual regifters : this affectation
was fneered at by moft of the Barrifters, who
well knew his fhallownefs; but, fuch as
gave themfelves the trouble of wafting a
thought on him were fomewhat furprized at
this new fpecies of vanity (as they imagined
it to be) and concluded, that the man was
lofing what little fhare of underftanding he
had. A fhort time, however, explained his
views. As foon as the death of Dr. Andrews was known, Blacquiere prevailed on
his inftrument, Lord Harcourt, to recommend Mr. Hutchinfon to his Majefty, as a
proper perfon to be appointed Provoft, in
Dr. Andrews's room; and he was accordingly appointed, to the univerfal aftonifhment of the kingdom, except Blacquiere and his accomplices. By this promotion the fecretary ferved the following
purpofes; as Mr. Hutchinfon, on being appointed Provoft, was, by compact, to refign
his two places of Alnager and Prime-ferjeant,
and refigned accordingly, Blacquiere kept
the

the Alnager's place to himself, the value of
* which I have already mentioned, and fatisfied the two candidates for the place of Solicitor-general, by appointing one Prime-ferjeant, and the other Solicitor. Thus was the-
Provoſtſhip, and (conſidering the exorbitant
powers of the Provoſt) the College publickly
fold, by the Secretary of a Lord Lieutenant,
to a perſon totally unqualified for the employment, (as I ſhall ſhew in the progreſs of
this work) for £1200 per ann. to himſelf,
and the opportunity of gratifying two gentlemen, who had demands on him for promotion, in the law line. I would not be
here underſtood to caſt the leaſt reflection on
theſe two gentlemen; I have a great perſonal
reſpect for both; and know them to be
eminently qualified for executing the duties of
their reſpective ſtations : would to God, that
all perſons promoted during the government
of Lord Harcourt (I ſhould have ſaid of
Blacquiere) had been as well qualified to diſ-
charge the duties of their reſpective employments ! I verily believe, if their intereſt
had been out of the queſtion, that the ſecre-
tary

---

* Blacquiere has ſince farmed out the Alnager's place at
£1200. per ann.

tary would have fold the Provoftfhip, for a lefs valuable confideration than £1200 per annum,. if he could not have procured a chapman to bid fo high; and that he would have fold it to a chimney-fweeper, if he had been the higheft bidder : I believe they had nothing to do with the fale, and that the promotion of one of them, at leaft, was only an incidental confequence of the fecretary's corruption in this particular. Mr. Hutchinfon, tho' he refigned two valuable places on this occafion, yet was a great gainer by the bargain: the income of the Provoftfhip is nearly two thoufand pounds annually, exclufive of the advantage of a very elegant habitation : the additional falary of £1000 per annum, which I have already mentioned to have been annexed to his office of Alnager, he did not refign with the place : for it was part of the bargain, that fome other place fhould be conferred on him, to which £1000 a year fhould be annexed as a falary; and that it fhould be a complete finecure : accordingly this was done : for there being a fmall port-town in the northern part of this kingdom, which confifts only of a few fifhermens huts, called Strangford, and there

having

having been heretofore a revenue-officer refident in it, called a fearcher, with an annual falary of £6 13s. 4d. Mr. Hutchinfon
was appointed *Searcher of the port of Strangford, with the falary of £1000 per ann.* for
his own life, and the lives of his *two* eldeft
fons. This appointment he preferred to a penfion of the fame value, for the fame term,
to avoid being one of the objects of the parliamentary railing of *fuch* patriots as he had
himfelf been, againft penfions and their pof-
feffors : but I have fome hopes, that this
artifice will not protect him from the cry of
the pack, for it is evident, that a penfion is
much lefs hurtful to the kingdom, than an
additional falary annexed to a place; as penfions expire with the grantees, but places and
their falaries exift for ever. Another great
advantage, which Mr. Hutchinfon propofed
to himfelf by this bargain, was, the power
of nominating two members of parliament :
this was his darling object; as he found parliamentary fervices were alone rewarded.
The two members, who are ufually called the
reprefentatives of the Univerfity, in parliament, are not elected by the members of the
Univerfity, that is, by all graduates above
the

the degree of a Batchelor of arts, who have commenced in this Univerſity; but they are elected by the Fellows and Scholars of the College only, and, therefore, are more proper-ly the repreſentatives of the College, than the Univerſity. The Fellows and Scholars, as I have already ſhewn, are ſubject to the ex-orbitant, ſtatutable, power of the Provoſt, and may be created by him : he therefore reckoned, with certainty, on his returning to parliament any two perſons, he ſhould think proper, as repreſentatives for the College. In this, however, his expectations have been fruſtrated, by the integrity, ſpirit, and good ſenſe of ſome members of the College.

It may not be amiſs, before I enter into the conſideration of the ruinous conſequences to learning, to religion, and conſequently to the whole nation, which muſt follow this infamous promotion, to obſerve, how far the Fellows and Scholars of the College have been wounded by it, as well in their proper-ties as in their dignity : and how little they deſerved ſuch unworthy treatment from his Majeſty's ſervants. The corporate body of the College conſiſts of twenty-two Fellows,

and

and feventy Scholars : the Fellows are chofen generally from amongft the Scholars, by the fuffrages of the Provoft, and feven Senior Fellows (unlefs the Provoft thinks fit to exert his power of nomination) after a publick and folemn examination, which lafts four days. They are all, except three, obliged by the ftatutes, and their oaths, to enter into holy orders: of thefe three, one is obliged, by the ftatutes, to profefs phyfick ; another common, and the third civil law. The Scholars are elected out of the body at large, after undergoing an examination likewife; and as, in thefe times, few perfons, unfupported by a parliamentary, or Englifh, intereft, can procure any preferments in this kingdom, unlefs thofe which it is in the power of the College to beftow, which are but few, and of no great value, College preferments, fuch as they are, have been generally fought after with avidity, by the learned, induftrious, and friendlefs. The venerable Prelate, and father of our church, who compiled the prefent ftatutes, had taken every precaution, which feemed, to his honeft foul, effectual for the prefervation of the ftream of preferment, in the College, pure and uncorrupted :

corrupted : befides ordaining, that ftrict and publick examinations fhould antecede every fpecies of Academick promotion, he had taken care, that the Electors fhould be bound, by the moft folemn oaths, to act impartially; and that thefe fhould be adminiftered to them kneeling, in the College-chapel, previous to each election. It is true, in thefe elective provifions, he had committed one capital error; which was, invefting the Provoft with the power of nomination : but, as he had obliged the Provoft to take the fame oath with the other Electors, his own integrity never fuffered him to fufpect, that any perfon, appointed to the government of a feminary, the chief end of whofe inftitution was, to promote religion and virtue, could be fo abandoned, as to break his oath; particularly when the breach muft be as publick as the examination, and merits, of the candidates. The fpirit of defpotifm, which evidently pervades the whole fyftem of the College ftatutes, has been a blemifh on the memory of this great Prelate : but when we confider the character of the times in which he lived, the obftinate faction he had to wreftle with, which embittered, and at laft deprived him

of,

of, his life, and make fome allowances for
his own natural warmth of temper, his too
great feverity of manners, and his want of
knowledge of the world, we may, perhaps,
find reafon, to think favourably of the fail-
ings of an honeft mind, whofe native integrity would not fuffer it to imagine, that
any perfon could pervert, to the worft purpofes, an exorbitant power, delegated to him
for the promotion of virtue only. Thus circumftanced, the College was the only afylum
for friendlefs merit in the kingdom. Each
of the fenior Fellows looked up at the Provoftfhip, as the higheft preferment, to whi h
he had ever any profpect of climbing ; and
as the hard-earned reward of his long labours
in the fervice of the publick. Each junior
Fellow waited, with impatience, for the happy hour of his fucceffion to a fenior Fellowfhip, which was to inveft him with academick power and pre-eminence, free him
from the inceffant toil and irkfome bondage,
which a tutor is fubject to, and give him a
provifion, ample in the eyes of a man, who
had been long ufed to fix them on no higher object. Every fcholar, who had dedicat-
ed his whole time, and, as it were, devoted
himfelf,

himſelf, to the ſtudy of the ſciences, expected, with ardour and anxiety, the glorious
and critical moment, when the vacancy of
a Fellowſhip gave him the opportunity of
diſplaying his abilities and learning, by ſuſtaining a publick examination with his fellow
candidates, before all the *literati* of the kingdom; and, perhaps, ſucceeding to a Fellowſhip, as the reward of his genius and
induſtry. Now, let us ſee, how all theſe
proſpects are darkened, and the property of
the Fellows, and Scholars, injured by the
promotion of Mr. Hutchinſon to the Provoſtſhip. Though the crown, by the new
charter and ſtatutes, as I have already ſaid,
retained to itſelf the power of nominating a
Provoſt, yet that power had been always,
previous to the nomination of Mr. Hutchinſon, exerciſed with prudence and diſcre-
tion. From the time of granting the new
charter and ſtatutes, to the time of his promotion, no perſon, in any conſiderable degree defective, in the qualifications required
in a Provoſt by theſe ſtatutes, except Dr.
Andrews (who, though a Layman, was a
ſenior Fellow of the College) was ever promoted to the Provoſtſhip. One *Winter* indeed,

deed, an independant preacher, yet epifco-
pally ordained, during the ufurpation of
Cromwell, was obtruded on the College as
Provoft; but, as he was not legally Provoft,
I do not rank him in the lift: and this inftance fhews, that even an arbitrary illiterate ufurper paid fuch refpect to the College
ftatutes, the interefts of learning, and what
he thought, or affected to think, religion,
as to promote a perfon to the government
of the College, whom he looked upon as a
fcholar, and a clerick. Before the grant of
the new charter and ftatutes, in the very
infancy of the College, in the year 1609,
thirteen years only after its foundation, Mr.
William Temple, a Layman, (afterwards
Sir William Temple, and one of the Mafters in Chancery) was elected Provoft by the
fenior Fellows, who then had the power of
electing a Provoft: but at this time there
was no ftatute enjoining that the Provoft
fhould be a Clergyman, and the College depended almoft for its very fubfiftence on the
bounty of the Crown: hence it was prudent
to elect for Provoft a perfon approved of by
government, whofe intereft might fecure to
the College its very exiftence, and obtain
further

further favours for it. The Provoftfhip was then more a poft of honour, than of profit; the College could fcarcely fubfift, and was by no means the object of court rapacity: and Mr. Temple was recommended, to the choice of the Fellows, by the famous arch-bifhop Ufher, the protector, guardian, and benefactor of the College, then in great credit with government, and was, befides, eminently qualified for the employment; having been a Fellow of King's College, Cambridge, and mafter of the free-fchool at Lincoln. He was father of Sir John Temple, mafter of the Rolls in Ireland.

I admit alfo, that, during the reigns of the Stuart line, fome perfons, who had never been Fellows of this College, but were, notwithftanding, Academicks, men of letters, and in holy orders, educated in the Univerfities of Oxford and Cambridge, have been promoted to the Provoftfhip of this College; but fuch promotions, tho' of men well qualified for the execution of the duty of the employment, have been uniformly complained of, as grievances to the College, and ought, in reafon, to be accounted fo. From

the

the time of the glorious revolution (at
which period, the principles of liberty and
property were better underſtood, and more
ably vindicated, than at any other preceding
period of our monarchy) to the time of Mr.
Hutchinſon's promotion, none, but Fellows of this College, have been promoted to the government of it, tho' there
have been, in that time, five ſucceſſive Pro-
voſts : ſo that I ſhall not heſitate to affirm,
that the Fellows of this College had a pre-
ſcriptive claim to the Provoſtſhip, founded
on an uninterrupted cuſtom, which had prevailed during the reigns of five of our moſt
glorious monarchs, and in the pureſt Era of
our conſtitution. I believe it will appear
too, that they have a claim founded on reaſon; for, no ſtranger, unacquainted with the
ſtatutes, rules, and cuſtoms of this College,
tho' a man of letters, can be reaſonably ſup-
poſed as capable of governing it, as a perſon,
who has paſſed almoſt his whole life in it,
and has been long exerciſed in obeying, as
well as enforcing obedience to, its ſtatutes,
rules and cuſtoms. The power of nominating a Provoſt, reſerved to the Crown, may
be fully exerted, without prejudice to theſe

two

two claims; for the nomination of the Sovereign, alone, can make a Provost; and he
may nominate him from amongst the Fellows. Neither will our present most gracious
Sovereign complain, that his power is
abridged, when it is circumscribed only by
his own reason and discretion. The great
alteration, made in the constitution of this
College, by the new charter and statutes, in
taking from the Fellows the power of electing their own Provost, and vesting it in the
Crown, was made, to prevent puritanism,
then the powerful, common, enemy of church
and state, from taking root in it, and to
attach the Fellows, and, by those means,
their pupils, to the interest of the crown
and constitution, by promoting such Fellows only, as were well affected to both, to
the government of the College; and not
with the view of totally ruining this Seminary, by appointing, for its Provosts, such
rapacious, illiterate minions, as every court
is, from time to time, infested with.

Having thus established the justice of the
claim of the Fellows to succeed to the Provostship, at least by prescription and reason,
the

the value of their lofs, as well as that of the Scholars, by the appointment of the prefent Provoft (without at all confidering the affront thrown upon them) may be eafily eftimated by the following calculation. Suppofing the annual income of the Provoft-fhip to be altogether £2100, that it was the right of fome one of the feven Senior Fellows to fucceed to it, on the death of the late Provoft, and that the chance of fucceffion, in each of the feven, was equal; the chance of each of the feven, on the late Provoft's death, was, on thefe data or principles, worth £300 per ann. for his life, but as the fucceffor muft have refigned his Senior Fellowfhip, worth, at the utmoft, one year with another, £700 per ann. £100 per ann. muft be deducted from the value of the chance of each, on this account : and then the value of the chance of each will ftand at £200 per ann. which, at ten years purchafe, the ufual fum paid for annuities for the lives of healthy perfons, amounts to £2000 fterl. thus, it is evident, that every Senior Fellow, by the appointment of the prefent Provoft, fuppo-fing their chances of fucceffion equal, loft £2000 fterl. and if any one of them had a greater profpect of fuccefs, than another, he

D   loft

loft more in proportion. The Senior of the
Junior Fellows, at a medium, remains two
years and upwards in that ftation, and, fuppofing the difference, between the annual income of a Senior and Junior Fellow, to
amount to £500, the Fellow, who was Senior of the Juniors, at the time of the appointment of the prefent Provoft, lofing, by
his appointment, the immediate fucceffion
into the place of fuch Senior Fellow, as
ought to have been appointed, thereby actually loft £1000; all the other Junior Fellows loft, by his appointment, in proportion to their rank and ftanding. By calculation, there are two Fellowfhips vacant, in
every period of three years; the fcholars,
therefore, who were prepared to offer themfelves candidates for vacant Fellowfhips,
loft, by his appointment, one prize, an object of their honourable contention : the
College was deprived of the power of providing for one man of abilities, and the induftry and learning of fome unfortunate indivi-
dual went unrewarded, to the mortification
and difcouragement of others, treading in
the fame laborious path of honeft Fame.
In the preceding calculation nothing is eftimated, but the quantum of the injury, in
point

point of property, fuſtained by ſuch Fellows and Scholars, as were Members of the
College, at the time of Mr. Hutchinſon's
appointment, by the ſingle Job in his favour. If the ruinous precedent ſhould be
followed by ſucceſſive governors of this kingdom, the eſtimation, of the damage to the ſociety, will be infinitely greater. Thus, the
only ſcanty proviſion and encouragement,
which depravity, almoſt univerſal, had ſuffered to remain in this kingdom, for modeſt,
friendleſs, literary merit, and languiſhing
religion, was invaded and plundered, by the
ſhameleſs rapacity of two men, equally mean,
avaricious, and illiterate; the enormity of
whoſe guilt is ſtill exaggerated by the reflection, that national ruin is the more certain conſequence of their corruption, than
the oppreſſion of individuals.

The indignity, with which the College
has been treated, on this occaſion, is next
to be conſidered ; and, ſurely, no greater
affront can be thrown on a body of men,
diſtinguiſhed for learning and piety, many
of them the brighteſt ornaments of the
church of Ireland, than ſo publick a declaration of their Sovereign, as the appointment

D 2 of

of Mr. Hutchinfon, to the Provoftſhip, feems to amount to, that there was not one amongſt them qualified to fuperintend the education of the youth of the kingdom, and their inſtruction in true religion and virtue. Such a character of the Fellows, of this unfortunate College, muſt have certainly been given to his Majeſty, or he never could have been induced to diſgrace a fet of as faithful fubjects, as can be found in any part of his dominions, by making fo very unuſual and extraordinary a promotion to their prejudice: but, I have already fet forth the cauſes, which induced the King's fervants here, probably, to forge fo infamous a miſrepreſentation of the College, with the character and views of the man, who procured it to be done : and I believe the impartial Publick will not think leſs reſpectfully of the members of the College, becauſe the venality of fuch a creature, as Blacquiere, has cauſed them to be diſgraced, inſulted, and oppreſſed. The proſperity and honour of this College has not always been fo ſlightly thought of by the Servants of the crown. I can, myſelf, remember *five* reverend Prelates, in this kingdom, at one time, who had all been Fellows

of

of the College, and who owed their promotion to the learning and piety they had difplayed, in the exercife of their duties there :
hard reverfe! not one perfon, who has been
a Fellow, now poffeffes any dignity or promotion in the church, except fuch preferments, as the poor patronage of the College
can beftow ; inftead of receiving favours
from the crown, they are defpoiled of the
only confiderable promotion, which they had
a right to expect, and the duties of which,
they, alone, are beft capable of difcharging.
It may be afked here, whether the prefent
Fellows had degenerated from the merit of
their predeceffors? whether they had encouraged, in any manner whatfoever, the fac-
tions, which now difturb part of his Majefty's dominions, or given any offence to the
crown, or its fervants here, fo as to provoke
the infliction of the heavy punifhment, which
has fallen upon them ?   All thefe queftions,
may truly be anfwered in the negative : a
great majority of the Fellows, at prefent in
this College, both Senior and Junior, are
perfons of as much fkill, in every branch of
learning, of as unblemifhed reputations, of
as found principles, in refpect to church and
ftate,

ftate, and of as unfhaken loyalty to his
Majefty, and his illuftrious houfe, as can be
found in any part of his dominions. The
borough could not have been more fafely, or
advantageoufly placed, for the real fervice
of the crown, than in their hands. They
had always returned, into parliament, fuch
members, as they thought firmly attached
to the intereft of their King and country;
and fuch, almoft without exception, as
were very agreeable to the King's fervants
here. His Majefty's attorney-general in Ireland, one of the greateft men which this
country has produced, and, perhaps, the
ableft and wifeft fervant of the crown, in this
kingdom, has been one of the reprefentatives
of this univerfity, for thefe thirty-nine
years paft. It was fo much the intereft, and
fo conftantly the practice, of the members of
this College, to return, for members, fuch
perfons, as might be faid to be nominated by
adminiftration, that no borough in the kingdom could be juftly counted more friendly
to government. So that, the fecuring the
borough, for the intereft of government,
could never be one of the reafons for the promotion of the prefent Provoft: and, if he
fhould

ſhould ever get this borough into his hands, which God forbid ! I'll venture to predict, that government will have ſufficient reaſon to repent the aſſiſtance it has afforded him, in that particular. His open threats of re-turning to his old trade of patriotizing, whenever he is refuſed a place (which often happens, his demands being as numerous as vacancies) ſhew, that I may, perhaps, turn out a true prophet; and, the deſertion of three voices, viz. of him, and the two members for the College; which, heretofore, were friends of government, may, ſometime or other, be a matter of conſequence to ad-miniſtration.

I ſhall here inſert all the arguments (if they may be ſo called) which have been made uſe of, by Mr. Hutchinſon, and his parti-ſans, to juſtify him in ſoliciting for, and adminiſtration in conferring on him, ſuch an employment ; not ſo much with the view of anſwering them (for they don't deſerve or require it) as to expoſe to the world the futility of any thing, which can be ſaid in ſupport of this ſcandalous meaſure : firſt, it is alleged, on behalf adminiſtration, that

the

the Provoſtſhip is one of the beſt employments in the gift of the crown here, and,
therefore, ought to be conferred, only, on
ſuch a perſon, as is able to do ſervice, by
his abilities and attendance in the houſe of
commons: now, ſuppoſing the Provoſtſhip to
be one of the beſt employments in the gift
of the crown, in this kingdom, which is
not the caſe, how can it from thence be in-
ferred, that it ought to be given to a member of the houſe of commons? is the influence of the crown ſo weak, in the houſe
of commons, of Ireland, that every thing
muſt be ſacrificed to ſtrengthen it? muſt religion, national advantage, nay, even the
common rules of juſtice and decency, be all
deſtroyed, betrayed, and ſubverted, to procure a majority there? is the lower houſe of
parliament an immenſe gulph, gaping to
ſwallow up all the realm, every thing, ſacred
and profane? is faction, of late, grown ſo
predominant therein, that the King's buſineſs cannot be carried on as heretofore? no:
the crown never had ſo powerful an influence, in the Iriſh houſe of commons, as at
preſent; the oppoſition in the laſt parliament,
for the two or three laſt ſeſſions of it, could

never

never muster one-fourth, seldom a sixth part, of the house under its banner; and, in all reasonable expectation, will not be near so strong in the present. Since the reign of Charles the first, no Provost, except the present, and his immediate predecessor, ever sat in the house of commons: and it was one of the shades, in the character of that amiable man, Dr. Andrews, that his ambition so far got the better of his sense of the duty he owed to the College, as to induce him to solicit for a seat in parliament, after he was appointed Provost; for he never sat in it before: and he strongly expressed his repentance for having done so, shortly before his death; probably, perceiving the ill use which would be made of the example he had set, by the greedy vultures about the court. If the inference, that all valuable employments should be conferred on members of the house of commons, be a good one, why are not all the archbishopricks, bishopricks, and church dignities in this kingdom, being valuable employments, conferred on members of the house of commons? the objection, that such employments can be only conferred on churchmen, who cannot sit in the
house

houfe of commons, lies equally againft the
difpofal of the Provoftfhip, to a member of
the houfe of commons ; for the ftatutes require, that the Provoft fhould be a church-
man, and a doctor, or, at leaft, a bachelor
in divinity ; but, I have dwelt too long on
this ridiculous argument, which has been referved to honour the fagacity of this generation, and never was thought of by our fore-
fathers, fince the foundation of the College.
I fhall only afk the reverend governors of
the two renowned univerfities of Oxford and
Cambridge, how they would refent the
crown's nomination of a practifing barrifter,
and member of the Englifh parliament, to
one of their moft valuable academick employments, for his fervices in the houfe of commons ; as for inftance, of Mr. Thurloe, or
Mr. Wedderburne, to the office of dean of
Chrift-church, in Oxford ? fuch a cafe
would be nearly fimilar to the prefent one ;
for the duty of the dean of Chrift-church,
in Oxford, is of the fame nature with the
duty of the Provoft of Trinity-college, Dublin ; and the crown has an equal right of
nomination to both places : but the Oxford
college would have much lefs reafon to complain,

plain, becaufe Meffrs. Thurloe and Wedderburne are both men of diftinguifhed abilities, learning and gentlemanly behaviour,
and therefore, in fome meafure, qualified
for the employment ; whereas the unhappy
Dublin college is tyrannized over by a governor, of whom it is hard to fay, whether he exceeds in ignorance, or infolence.
I dare affirm, that the injured univerfity
would take fire at fuch treatment. The noble ftand made by Magdalen college, when
that furious bigot, James the Second, would
have obtruded the bifhop of Oxford on it, as
prefident, fhews the fpirit, which at that
time animated the univerfity of Oxford ; and
we have no reafon to fuppofe, that either of
the univerfities of Oxford, or Cambridge,
would fupport their rights now, with lefs
vigour and fpirit, if they were invaded.

It is next alleged, on behalf of Mr. Hutchinfon, that if he had not been promoted
to the place of Provoft, one Mr. Flood
would have obtained it. I know nothing of
Mr. Flood, except that he is a perfon, the
fervice of whofe abilities, in parliament, adminiftration, in the reign of Blacquiere, has
thought

thought fit to purchafe, by giving him the very lucrative and honourable employment of one of the vice-treafurers of Ireland. Now this argument, in favour of Mr. Hutchinfon, if it means any thing, means this; that Blacquiere was determined to make the moft of the place, and that if Mr. Hutchinfon had not bid for it, the fecretary would have found his advantage, fome way or other, in giving it to Mr. Flood, who would not have made as good a Provoft as Mr. Hutchinfon. For, if it is allowed, that he would have made as good, or a better Provoft than Mr. Hutchinfon, he can derive no advantage whatfoever to his caufe, from the argument. Suppofing the fact to be, that if Mr. Hutchinfon had not, Mr. Flood would have been appointed Provoft, the truth of which refts only on the affertions of Mr. Hutchinfon's partifans, how does this excufe Mr. Hutchinfon's avarice and prefumption, in feeking for fuch a preferment. It would be no good plea, for a robber, at the bar, to allege, that, if he had not committed a robbery, another would : but the implication, that Mr. Flood would not have made as good a

Provoft,

Provoſt, as Mr. Hutchinſon, is by no means
to be endured ; for every perſon in the kingdom, of good manners, and a reaſonable
portion of underſtanding (and it is not alleged, on behalf of Mr. Hutchinſon, that
Mr. Flood is defective in theſe particulars)
would have made a better Provoſt than Mr.
Hutchinſon.

The only other argument, which I have
heard uſed in behalf of Mr. Hutchinſon, is,
that an Engliſhman would have been appointed Provoſt, if he had not ; this, if
true, may receive pretty nearly the ſame anſwer, with the foregoing ; but as its truth
reſts only on the bare aſſertions of Mr.
Hutchinſon's partiſans, and as it carries little probability with it, I can't ſay I give
credit to it : yet, as of two evils the leſſer
is always to be preferred, if it had been determined by adminiſtration, to diminiſh the
already ſcanty encouragement for literary
merit in this kingdom, and to inſult and injure the members of the college, by ſlight-
ing their claim of ſucceſſion to the Provoſtſhip, a clergyman, and a member of one of
the univerſities of Oxford or Cambridge,
would

would have been the propereſt perſon to have been appointed Provoſt, for many rea- ſons needleſs to mention; and, whether Clerick or Layman, he muſt have been a very bad man indeed, if he would not have made a better Provoſt than the preſent.

Having thus completed the firſt part of my deſign, that is, faithfully explained to the publick the means by which Mr. Hutchin- ſon procured the Provoſtſhip, I ſhall begin the ſecond part of it, to wit; the inquiry whether he is capable of performing the du- ties of that ſtation, with an exact tranſlation of the ſecond chapter of the college ſtatutes, concerning the quality and duty of the Pro- voſt, which is as follows, " The conſtituti-
" on of a body politick requires, in the firſt
" place, that a proper head be appointed,
" by whom the other members may be di-
" rected to the common good of the whole
" body. We therefore ordain, that the
" Provoſt be a man *of ſound morals, exem-*
" *plary life, and unblemiſhed reputation; at*
" *leaſt thirty years old, and in holy orders,*
" *and that he be a doctor or at leaſt a bache-*
" *lor in divinity.* All other qualifications
" being

" being equal, let a man educated in the
" college be preferred to a foreigner; and
" let him not poſſeſs or accept of (as long
" as he fills the place, and performs the du-
" ty of Provoſt,) more than one eccleſiaſti-
" cal benefice, with cure of ſouls : but we
" do not intend to prohibit him, by this laſt
" clauſe, from poſſeſſing, or accepting of
" any eccleſiaſtical dignity, below a Biſhop-
" rick, ſo that he keeps due reſidence as
" Provoſt, and performs all other parts of
" his duty, according to the ſtatutes of the
" college. Let him be provident in his fa-
" mily affairs; and let him manage the eſ-
" tate, and tranſact the buſineſs of the col-
" lege, in ſuch a manner, that he may ap-
" pear to ſeek the advantage of the college,
" and not his own : and let him not obey
" the dictates of favour, hatred, or any other
" paſſion of the mind, in examining into,
" or adjudging cauſes, but let him always
" be guided by equity. To him we com-
" mand all the Fellows, Scholars, and Ser-
" vants of the college, in their order, to be
" ſubject ; and to obey him, without mur-
" muring, in all things lawful and honeſt,
" which regard ſcholaſtick exerciſe, or the
                                        " government,

" government, advantage, or honour of the
" college. Let him take care of all the of-
" ficers, and lecturers, and especially of the
" Dean and Bursar; and if he finds them
" defective, or negligent, in the perform-
" ance of their duty, let him punish them
" according to his pleasure; unless where
" the statutes expressly define the punish-
" ment for such fault. In the same man-
" ner, wherever, in these statutes, any thing
" is commanded or forbidden to any of the
" *students,* of whatsoever rank, or to the of-
" ficers and servants of the College, or any
" of them, without a penalty being annex-
" ed, or, where a penalty is annexed, with-
" out mention of the person, who is to in-
" flict it, the Provost shall take care, that
" the performance of the duty be enforced
" by a proper punishment, and that the pre-
" scribed punishment be inflicted. *And we*
" *ordain, that the Provost shall remain in his*
" *office, as long as he shall behave himself well*
" *and honestly,* and live according to the or-
" dinances of these statutes. We ordain al-
" so, that no person be elected Provost, un-
" less he is an unmarrried man; and if it
" shall so happen, that he should marry af-
" ter

" ter his election, that he resign his place,
" or be actually removed from the College."
Many other qualifications required in the
Provoſt, and branches of his duty, beſides
thoſe recited in this chapter, appear in different parts of the ſtatutes, and particularly
in his oath; but I ſhall defer the recital of
this oath, 'till I come to the third part of
my taſk, to wit, the account of Mr. Hutchinſon's conduct in the government of the
College, that the reader may have an opportunity of comparing his conduct, with that
preſcribed by the Provoſt's oath. From this
chapter it appears, that the Provoſt ought
to be a Doctor or Bachelor in Divinity, and
an unmarried man; but the crown exerted
the power of diſpenſation, reſerved to it by
the new charter and ſtatutes, in theſe two
particulars, in favour of Mr. Hutchinſon,
who was not a Doctor or Bachelor in Divinity, nor an unmarried man. Before I make
any obſervations on this diſpenſation, I ſhall
recite Mr. Hutchinſon's defects, in reſpect
to the other qualifications required in a Provoſt by the ſtatutes. That he is not a man of
exemplary life, or unblemiſhed reputation,
is well known to the world, and will appear

E   clearly

clearly in the sequel of this work : it will also appear, that he is not provident, nor œconomical; that he does not manage the estate, nor transact the businefs, of the College, in such a manner as to appear to seek the advantage of the College, and not his own, but in a manner directly contrary; that in examining into, and adjudging causes, he does not follow the rules of equity, and that he is not capable of doing so; but follows the dictates of the most inveterate malice, extravagant folly, and unbridled fury; being totally under the guidance of the most turbulent, and malignant paffions. Every member of the College is bound to obey the Provoft, in all things lawful and honeft, in refpect to *fcholaftick exercife;* and it is a branch of his duty, to infpect into the conduct of the officers and lecturers, and, if he finds them defective, or negligent, in the performance of their duty, to punifh them according to his pleafure; thus it appears, that the Provoft ought to be a man of learning, and the neceffity of his being fo I fhall hereafter demonftrate: but I fhall alfo fhew, that Mr. Hutchinfon is ridiculoufly illiterate, even more fo than could be expected,

confidering

confidering his profeffion : 'tis true Mr.
Hutchinfon received part of his education
in this College, and is above thirty years of
age, and had, fo far, two qualifications for
the Provoftfhip, required by the ftatutes;
but thefe are the only qualifications, of all
required, which he is poffeffed of; and how
far they entitled him to this promotion, let
all the world judge. With refpect to the
difpenfation granted to Mr. Hutchinfon, it
is proper to obferve, that nothing could be
more prejudicial to the intereft, nay to the
very defign and end, of the inftitution of the
College. It was at firft inftituted, as I have
already mentioned, for the purpofe of diffuf-
ing the true light of the gofpel, in this kingdom, by educating, and providing for the
future education of a learned and pious minif-
try; and for this reafon, the venerable compiler of the prefent ftatutes had wifely provided, that a divine fhould prefide over it;
thinking it an abfurdity of the groffeft kind,
to permit a layman to be the principal in-
ftructor of the growing church, in this
realm : not that all laymen are incapable of
being fo, but becaufe it is infinitely more
probable, that the perfons, who have made

E 2   divinity

divinity the ftudy, and piety the practice of their lives, are abler to inftruct the rifing generation, in the fublime myfteries of our holy religion, and to ftimulate them, by their example, to the exercife of all the duties of it, than men, whofe different views in life have directed them to other ftudies and employments. He had alfo wifely provided, that the Provoft fhould be an unmarried man, and, if he thought proper to marry, that he fhould refign his place : becaufe, as he had given him exorbitant power, by the ftatutes, over the eftate, property, and emoluments of the College, he thought a bachelor, having no family of his own to provide for, would look on the College as his family ; and would alfo have lefs allurements to wafte the property of the college, and divert the emoluments of it from their original ufe and defign, than a married man, who might be induced to do fo, for the advancement and profit of his Family, and children : thus, taking every precaution, to guard againft the infirmity or depravity of the human heart. Of the wifdom of this laft provifion we have had fufficient proofs, by the bequefts of Provofts Baldwin and
Andrews,

Andrews to the College. It never entered into the thoughts of this holy Prelate, that the power of difpenfation, which, as well as the power of nomination to the Provoftfhip, he was referving to the crown, with the defign already mentioned, in treating of the power of nomination, would, by the mediation of corrupt and wicked men, be one day or other exercifed, to deftroy thofe wife provifions, and thereby overturn this, his favourite feminary. It is alleged, in juftification of this difpenfation to Mr. Hutchinfon, that his predeceffor, Dr. Andrews, had alfo a difpenfation, which excufed his want of the qualifications of being a clerick, and a doctor, or bachelor in divinity : to this it may be anfwered, firft, that it is no defence of a wicked and ruinous meafure, to fhew, that the like has been done in one, or even many inftances already ; and fecondly, that the cafes of Dr. Andrews, and Mr. Hutchinfon, are widely different. Dr. Andrews, as I have already fhewn, had almoft every qualification to entitle him to the Provoftfhip, except the fingle one of being a clerick : I admit his enemies accufed him of being too much the bon vivant, or good-
fellow,

fellow, and complained of his conduct in private life, as somewhat too loose and unguarded for a Provost: malice itself laid nothing else to his charge; and perhaps the accusation may be, in some degree, true, tho' greatly exaggerated. His behaviour, however, in the College, was decent and regular, and, as a man of integrity and honour, his character was unexceptionable: he was a man of letters, and a Senior Fellow of the College, at the time he was appointed Provost, and then was, and continued 'till his death, unmarried. At the time of his promotion, he was a practising Barrister, but immediately afterwards quitted the bar, to attend to the duties of his station; he had also regularly obtained the degree of doctor of laws: so that however religion was injured by his promotion, the College and its members were neither insulted nor injured by it; nor were the interests of learning sacrificed: let us now review the account on the side of Mr. Hutchinson; Mr. Hutchinson possesses no qualification for the provostship, except the two very trifling ones already mentioned, and he has obtained a dispensation to excuse

his

his defect, not in one, but in two of the most
neceffary, and in their nature indifpenfible,
qualifications of a Provoft, to wit, clericifm
and celibacy ; he is encumbered with a very
numerous family of children, fome of whom,
as it may be reafonably prefumed, from
what I fhall hereafter mention, he intends
to quarter on the eftate of the College, his
income being inadequate to his expenfes notwithftanding his immenfe appointments ; fo
that the character of *alieni appetens fui profu-
fus* was not more applicable to Cataline,
than it is to him. The College-walks and
gardens, heretofore facred to the exercife and
contemplation of the fober academick, are
now infefted by himfelf and military officers
mounted on prancing horfes; his wife and
adult daughters, with their train of female
companions, and his infant children, their
nurfes and go-carts ; who by their pomp and
clamour have banifhed the mufes, and may
probably be the authors of greater and more
ferious evils : He is entirely illiterate, and
was not a Fellow, or any member of the
College, at the time of his promotion, nor
was any degree, fuperior to that of Bachelor of arts, ever conferred on him by the
University,

Univerſity, to which he was entitled by
learning and attendance: for the degree of
doctor of laws, which he has obtained, was
an honorary one, the nature of which I
ſhall preſently explain; ſo that not only
religion was wounded, but every member
of the College was inſulted, as well as injured, by his appointment, and the intereſts
of learning and the nation ſacrificed. At the
time of his promotion to the Provoſtſhip, he
was a practiſing Barriſter, but has not, like
Doctor Andrews, quitted the bar, on his
promotion, ſtill attending there with the
ſame avidity as before, altho' the attendance
neceſſary, in the exerciſe of that profeſſion,
is incompatible with the execution of his
duty as Provoſt, ſuppoſing he was capable
of executing it. Every member of the
Iriſh parliament, learned or unlearned, has,
by cuſtom, a right to have an honorary degree in law conferred on him by the univerſity: this degree is merely complimentary;
no academick exerciſes whatſoever are to be
performed for it; the learning of the candidate is never inquired into; he pays no
fees to the Univerſity; nor do ſuch degrees
entitle a man to any privileges: ſuch is the
degree

degree by which Mr. Hutchinfon (for I never give the title of doctor to an honorary one) affumes the privilege of writing L. L. D. after his name, and this degree he obtained, fhortly after an ignorant carpenter, one John Magill (whofe character is well known in this kingdom, and who had been thruft into the houfe of commons by a powerful nobleman,) obtained the honorary degree of doctor of laws. I cannot give my readers jufter ideas of the proftitution of thefe honorary degrees; of the cheapnefs in which they are held; and of the ignorance of fome perfons on whom they are conferred, than by telling them, that, whilft I was royal profeffor of civil law in the univerfity of Dublin, I officially prefented Blacquiere himfelf to the univerfity, and that he was made an honorary doctor of laws; yet there is the ftrongeft reafon to fuppofe, that Mr. Hutchinfon was recommended to his Majefty, as equally qualified for the employment of Provoft with Dr. Andrews; for the gazette, which announced Mr. Hutchinfon's promotion to the Provoftfhip, fet it forth in the following terms: " His Majefty has been " pleafed to appoint the right honourable
                                    " John

" John Hely Hutchinson, L. L. D. Provost
" of Trinity College Dublin, in the room
" of the right honourable. Francis An-
" drews, L. L. D. deceafed." If fo infamous
a fraud was ufed (and fraud of fome kind
certainly was made ufe of in the tranfaction,)
to induce his Majefty to promote Mr. Hutchinfon to fo important a poft, the con-
trivers of it deferve not only the abhorrence
of the whole nation, but the moft exemplary punifhment. When I reflect on the
abfurdity and indecency of the promotions
in Ireland, during the unhappy lieutenancy
of this driveling patron of Blacquiere, I can't
help being furprifed, that Blacquiere did
not procure the Provoftfhip for himfelf.
It is a lucrative employment, he was a
member of parliament, full as poor and greedy, and as well qualified for the place, as
his friend Hutchinfon: he had as good an
L. L. D. at the end of his name, and, as
he was not a knight at the time of the late
Provoft's death, his promotion would have
made the fame figure in the gazette. Let us
fee how it wou'd ftand : " His Majefty has
" been pleafed to appoint the right honour-
" able John Blacquiere, L. L. D. Provoft of
" Trinity

" Trinity College, Dublin, in the room of
" the right honourable Francis Andrews,
" L. L. D. deceafed." *Mutato nomine de
te Fabula narratur*; there is no difference
but in the name.

I have already fhewn, from the fecond
chapter of the ftatutes, how neceffary a qualification learning is for a Provoft : indeed,
without deducing the neceffity of fuch a
qualification, for the Provoftfhip, from any
quotations of the ftatutes, reafon wou'd dictate to every one, that a man placed at the
head of a feminary, inftituted for the exprefs purpofe of inftructing the youth of a
whole kingdom in all the various branches
of literature, ought to be the moft learned
man, who cou'd be procured, after diligent and exact inquiry : but by the reca-
pitulation of fome moft extraordinary and
exorbitant powers, given to the Provoft of
the College, I fhall fhew that learning, of
the fublimeft and abftrufeft kind, is a more
neceffary qualification in the Provoft of this
College, than in the head of any learned
feminary in Europe.   The Provoft, as I
have already mentioned, is by the ftatutes
empowered

empowered to nominate the Fellows, after
the candidates for vacant Fellowſhips have
undergone a publick examination, by himſelf and the ſeven Senior Fellows, and after
an election made by the examiners; which
election (if he nominates) I have already
ſhewn to be nugatory ; now the examination
of the candidates for Fellowſhips, in the
College of Dublin, may, without exaggeration, be pronounced the ſevereſt, the moſt
ſolemn, and critical, eſtabliſhed at this Day
on any part of the earth. If there is a vacancy of a Fellowſhip, this examination begins
annually on the Wedneſday preceding
Trinity Sunday : a large theatre, capable of
containing five hundred perſons, is previ-
ouſly erected in the College-hall : This theatre is crowded with the learned, not only
of the univerſity of Dublin, but of the
whole Kingdom. The ſituation of the
College in the midſt of a very great capital
city, the largeſt in Chriſtendom, except
London and Paris, giving the literati, as one
may ſay, of the whole nation an opportunity
of attending this examination, and whilſt
it continues, the doors of the hall are open
to every perſon of a gentlemanly appearance.

*
On

On one fide of an area, in the midft of this theatre, fit the Provoft and the feven Senior Fellows; oppofite to them, in the fame area, fit the candidates, and, as the area is at leaft fifteen feet wide, the diftance between the examiners and the candidates is fo great, that both the queftion and anfwer muft be pronounced in founds loud enough to be heard by the whole affembly; fo that all the learned prefent are able to form a judgment, as well of the fkill of the examiners, as of the learning of the candidates: This examination continues four days, for four hours each day, two in the morning, and two in the afternoon; during which time, the candidates are examined, with the moft critical feverity, in logick; in all the branches of mathematical learning; in natural and moral philofophy; in chronology, hiftory, and the learned languages; and their fkill in compofition in latin profe and verfe is alfo inquired into; the Provoft and each of the feven Senior Fellows examining different branches. Happy is the candidate, whom five years of moft intenfe application and ftudy, together with the inftructions of fome of the ableft profeffors in the King's dominions, can qualify to fuf-

tain

tain this examination with credit and fuccefs. Seven years generally, and often ten,
of the moft precious part of a man's life, are
confumed in this arduous purfuit, and the
healths of many have been fatally wafted
in it; the haggard, pallid countenances,
and meagre bodies, of the candidates, at the
time of examination, are fufficient proofs of
their antecedent labour and confinement, and
prefent anxiety : their reputations, as well
as future fubfiftence in life, being at
ftake. Such an ordeal muft every man pafs
through to a Fellowfhip, the fcanty and precarious reward of his toil. The Provoft, as
I before obferved, is obliged himfelf to examine, on this folemn trial ; it is in his power to nominate the Fellow from among the
candidates, tho' all the Senior Fellows
fhould vote againft the perfon, nominated by
him : he is alfo folemnly fworn to nominate,
or agree to the election of the moft merito-
rious candidate ; the Provoft therefore, to
qualify himfelf to perform his duty according to his oath, ought to be a perfon of
greater learning (if fuch can be found) than
any of the feven Senior Fellows ; becaufe
he is not only one of the examiners, but, by
his

his power of nomination, fole judge of the merit of the candidates, and able to control and over-rule the judgments of all his co-examiners together. Now let us fee, whether Mr. Hutchinfon be capable of performing this part of his duty: And, very happily, his own vanity and folly have given me an opportunity of demonftrating to the world, that he is quite unacquainted with the two learned languages of Greek and Latin; a fkill in which bounds even his own pretenfions to literature. An illiterate dunce, the very memory of whom in the college (as of Mr. Hutchinfon) had been worn out by length of time, if obtruded in the fame manner on the college, might, by the fingle faculty of difcretion, have efcaped with only the fufpicion of ignorance: a prudent taciturnity and referve, and a well-timed fit of the gout, or other ficknefs, are fufficient to preferve a Provoft from the too curious infpection of the inferior members of the college into his literary abilities: But Mr. Hutchinfon's petulance, and difpofition to mountebanking, very fhortly after his appointment, fully difcovered to the members of the college, his profound ignorance, even

of

of the commoneſt claſſicks ; as I ſhall prove
by an inſtance or two of his behaviour. I
was, at the time of his appointment, the ſecond of the Junior Fellows, and ſhortly after, during the abſence of two Senior Fellows,
was called up to be a member of the board,
as the ſtatutes direct : during my attendance
there, Mr. Hutchinſon, who ſeemed to
think, that the members of the board had
nothing to do, but to liſten to his frothy harangues, pronounced a ſpeech, which laſted
for an enormous length of time ; I think,
two hours, by my watch ; and had it not
been for the interruption I ſhall preſently
mention, it would probably have laſted two
hours longer. An hour and half of this time
were conſumed in paying us the moſt fulſome
compliments, in reſpect of the excellency of
our College-courſe, for the education of ſuch
as were committed to our care ; and was intended to reconcile us (for at his firſt coming
amongſt us, he thought it worth ſome pains
to keep us in temper) to an actual arraign-
ment of our conduct, in reſpect to this very
courſe of education, which he was laviſhly
praiſing. In the latter part of his harangue
he told us, tho' we took great pains to in-
ſtruct

ftruct the ftudents in the fciences, that we did
not exert equal attention in inftructing them
in the clafficks. It may be proper here to
remark, that this cenfure was founded on
ignorance and falfehood, and that he had
learned it from the groundlefs reports of the
vulgar and illiterate. The undergraduates
being obliged to read moft of the Latin and
Greek clafficks, previous to their obtaining
their degrees, as Bachelors of arts; and the
bachelors, before they become Mafters,
being alfo; in the courfe of their attendance
on the Greek lecturer, obliged to read the remaining and moft difficult clafficks; fo that
the diligent ftudents, of pregnant parts,
have as great incitements to, and opportunities of, acquiring, and actually do acquire,
as great knowledge of the two learned languages in this College, as in any other feminary whatfoever : For the ignorance of
the idle and ftupid, its members are not ac-
countable. In the progrefs of his harangue
he told us, that, at Eaton-college (which
is juftly celebrated as a fchool, to prepare
gentlemen for the Univerfitys) more pains
were taken to inftruct the Scholars, and
that they were actually better fkilled in the

F   learned

learned languages, than the ſtudents in the College of Dublin ; and to prove this, he introduced the example of his own ſon, of whoſe literary abilities, as well as of his own, he was deſirous to impreſs us with very high ideas. He told us, that before his ſon went to Oxford (for previous to his own promotion his ſon was no member of this College, nor would he now be ſo, but for electioneering purpoſes, as I ſhall hereafter ſhew) and whilſt he was yet a ſchool-boy at Eaton, when he came to viſit him in Dublin, in a long vacation, he opened the famous oration of Demoſthenes, concerning the crown, put it into his ſon's hand, and deſired him to tranſlate ſome pages of it into Engliſh ; which he readily performed, although, on inquiry, he told him, that he had never read the book before. This part of his harangue excited the indignation of a very learned member of the board ſo far, that he immediately interrupted him, and told him, that if he had been informed of ſo very extraordinary a circumſtance, by a leſs reſpectable authority, he would give very little credit to it : as he found it very diffi-cult to bring himſelf to believe, that a

ſchool-boy

fchool-boy could explain, at fight, without any ftudy or preparation, a book, which had exercifed, and, in fome particulars, baf- fled the fagacity of the moft learned criticks, fince the revival of letters in Europe; at the fame time mentioning the names of feveral of them. Mr. Hutchinfon, whofe vanity and ignorance never fuffered him to imagine, that he would meet with fo farcaftick a re- buke, of the poignancy of which he was not capable of being fully fenfible, was how- ever thrown into apparent confufion by it; and, after taking a confiderable time to re- collect himfelf, at length ftammered out, that he did not mean to affert, that his fon had critically explained the oration; and, turning to the gentleman, added, " Doctor, " you know that a perfon may get through " two or three pages of that book, without " meeting with any of thefe difficulties " which you mention :" " No, replied the " Doctor, determined to chaftize his igno- " rance, the difficulties in that book are thick- " er fet, than the ftars in the firmament." This reply had the defired effect; his agita- tion could be no longer concealed; the ha- rangue ended : and the board was difmiffed.

Sic

Sic nos servavit.—Now I would afk any gentleman, acquainted with this oration of Demofthenes, whether this ftory, which I
have faithfully related, without the leaft exaggeration, does not demonftrably prove,
that Mr. Hutchinfon had never read this oration, and had but little fkill in the Greek
tongue? For the fake of thofe only, who
are unlearned in Greek, I fhall take fome
pains to explain the nature of this proof.
The oration of Demofthenes, concerning
the crown, is an anfwer to the oration of
another famous orator, named Æfchines,
who accufed one Ctefiphon, of having
tranfgreffed the laws of Athens, in propo-
fing that a golden crown fhould be decreed
to Demofthenes, by the Athenians, for certain publick fervices. In handling this fubject, both in the accufation and defence,
thefe two great men, whofe art and eloquence were unequalled in their age, exerted
their utmoft abilities; in fact, the fubject
was too important to be flightly handled by
either one or the other; as the ruin of one of
them was, from circumftances not neceffary
here to relate, to be the confequence of the
conteft: now, from the very nature of the
fubject,

subject, both orations are full of quotations
and conftructions of the laws of Athens,
technical terms, and references to its local
cuftoms ; fo that, without ftudy or preparation, and a knowledge of the fubject, particularly of the Athenian laws and police, it
is impoffible for the beft Greek fcholar to
explain, or tranflate, either the one, or the
other : and the defence, to wit the oration
of Demofthenes, is more difficult to tranflate, in fuch circumftances, than the accufation. According to the prefent mode of
education, both in England and Ireland, no
man makes any confiderable proficiency in
the Greek tongue, without having read thefe
two orations : and hence it is plain, when
Mr. Hutchinfon told this ftory, relative to
his fon, that he was entirely unfkilled in the
Greek language. In vain will his partifans
endeavour to defend him, by afferting, that
the fon, to enhance his merit with his father,
might have deceived him, by telling him,
that he had never before read this oration ;
tho' he really had read it, before his father
examined him : for, fuppofing the fact to
be fo, it by no means invalidates the proof
of Mr. Hutchinfon's want of fkill in Greek ;
which

which refts entirely on his having publickly
afferted, in an affembly of learned men, that
his fon explained the oration, without having
even read it before. His fuppofing, or be-
lieving, that a fchool-boy (or any perfon
whatfoever) could tranflate that oration,
without having previoufly ftudied it, is an
inconteftable proof of his ignorance of the
Greek language : and he certainly believed it,
or he never would have afferted it, as a fact,
within his own knowledge, when the abfurdity and the impoffibility of it muft be ri-
diculed by every man of letters. This affectation of learning too, which, it is plain,
he did not poffefs, muft induce a fufpicion,
if we wanted certain proof, that he pretended to knowledge in other particulars,
with as little foundation to fupport his pretenfions.

I fhall now prefent my readers with another inftance of his behaviour, to prove his
ignorance of letters ; and, whether we confider the impudence or folly he difplayed in
it, I believe, it will be admitted by all, that
he is, in both, unrivalled. I have already
given an account of the folemnity of the examination,

amination, which candidates for vacant Fellowſhips are obliged to ſuſtain, and the various branches of learning, in which they are examined : how then muſt it aſtoniſh every perſon to hear, that Mr. Hutchinſon, confeſſedly ignorant of all the ſciences, and pretending only to a knowledge of Greek and Latin, had the matchleſs aſſurance to ſit as Provoſt, as Examiner, and as Judge of the merits of the candidates for the firſt Fellow-ſhip, which became vacant after his appoint-ment, in the preſence of ſo many of the learn-ed in this kingdom ! mountebanks generally erect their ſtages amongſt the populace; their tricks are deſigned only to deceive the vulgar and ignorant ; they know their trade, and the places proper to exerciſe it in : this man erected his ſtage in the very manſion of ſcience, and had the preſumption, or rather folly, to imagine, that his juggling would impoſe on the wiſe and learned : his beha-viour, however, in the Provoſt's chair, on this occaſion, has met with condign puniſh-ment, if contempt and ridicule are puniſh-ments. He aſſumed the province of ex-amining the candidates in the Greek language; the uſual method, heretofore practiſed by the

perſon

perfon appointed to examine Greek, was this:
the examiner took with him into the hall
fome Greek claffick, of eftablifhed reputation ; this book he put into the hands of
the candidates fucceffively, and they tranflated fuch parts of it, as the examiner thought
proper, who alfo, at intervals, took the
opportunity of inquiring into their critical
knowledge of the language. Mr. Hutchinfon was not contented with this mode of examination ; he intended, not fo much, to
gain a knowledge of the merits of the candidates, as to acquire immortal fame, in letters, to himfelf ; and with this view, tho'
he carried the Iliad into the hall, yet he
had collected a fet of queftions of a very extraordinary nature, all which he propofed to
the candidates, before he put the book into
their hands. Thefe queftions were fo contrived, that, tho' each of them took two mi-
nutes in the recital, the anfwer could not
poffibly confift of more than one word, either yes, or no ; or the name of fome poet,
hiftorian, or philofopher. Each of the queftions recited the character of fome great ancient, and then contained the demand of,
" guefs who that was ?" or, " was it not
" fuch

" fuch a man ?" In this new mode of examination he proceeded, with the loudeſt vo-
ciferation, the moſt ſolemn pomp, and without bluſh or heſitation ; ſo that he ſeemed,
and I verily believe he was, totally inſenſible
of the ridiculous abſurdity of his conduct,
and fancied himſelf gaining the applauſe and
veneration of an *audience*, impatient to crown
him with never-fading laurels. At length,
a ſtudent of the college, who had been an
Eaton ſcholar, informed the perſon who ſat
next to him, that the Provoſt was repeating
whole pages of the little art of rhetorick,
which was taught, at Eaton, to the boys
on the loweſt form : the ſtory ſpread, the
book was procured, and the ſtudent's aſſertion appeared to be literally true. This
little book, or pamphlet, is printed by one
Pote, at Eaton, and is entitled, *Elementa*
Rhetorica, in uſum juventutis Etonienſis,
cum excerptis ex Quintiliano, et Cicerone
de oratore. The chapter of this treatiſe,
which contained theſe *excerpta,* Mr. Hutchinſon had gotten by heart, and retailed
this ſmall ware with the utmoſt liberality
to the candidates and audience ; never ima-
gining, that the petit larceny would be de-
tected.

tected. I suppofe the pamphlet was recommended to his perufal by the learned Eatonian, who had, according to his account,
tranflated Demofthenes *peri Stephanou,* by
intuition. It cannot be alleged, with any
appearance of truth, or probability, that Mr.
Hutchinfon had reforted to the original authors, Quintilian and Cicero, and from them
collected his queftions ; becaufe his memory
was fo unluckily tenacious on this occafion,
that he went through the whole chapter of
Pote's pamphlet, in the exact order obferved
therein, and did not omit even an *et,* or an
etiam, or any particle whatfoever, inferted
in it ; but repeated it with admirable accuracy, adding only, now and then, when he
had rehearfed half a page, *Quifnam fuit hic ?*
or, *Nonne talis fuit Homerus, Pindarus,*
&c ? Any perfon, who can affert that
he had reforted to the original authors,
muft firft take it for granted, that he, and
the compiler of Pote's pamphlet, had agreed
fo exactly in tafte, as to adopt the very fame
paffages in thefe two Authors ; a wonderful *Hypothefis* indeed ! Whenever he ventured to infert the fmalleft addition of his own,
he manifefted fo entire an ignorance of even
the

the firſt rudiments of grammar, that ſome ſchool-boys, ſitting on the upper and remote benches, cou'd not contain their laughter. *Quo Periodo*, and like attacks on Priſcian's head, were common with him. * Excluſive of the injury and affront to theſe unfortunate candidates, in having ſo ignorant a perſon appointed to be judge of their abilities and literary acquirements, the College ſuſtained the moſt material damage, in having the ſolemn examination for Fellowſhips, the glorious ſupport of its reputation in the republick of letters, degraded, debaſed, and made a ſubject for ridicule, by the folly and vanity of an illiterate mummer.

I cou'd recite other innumerable inſtances of his conduct, all tending to the ſame point; but I think the two I have mentioned ſufficient

---

* To make his ignorance and folly, if poſſible, more mani-feſt, I ſhall recite one very ridiculous anecdote, concerning his behaviour on this occaſion : he aſked one of the candi-dates, in very bad latin, " At what period eloquence flouriſh-ed moſt amongſt the Greeks ?" The candidate, not knowing the proper anſwer, after ſome deliberation, anſwered by gueſs, " In the time of the Peloponneſian war." Here the candidate, in his turn, puzzled the Provoſt ; the book, out of which he had taken the queſtion, had informed him, that eloquence
flouriſhed

cient to convince the most incredulous, that
he has not the slightest tincture of learning,
even in that branch, of which alone he pre-
tends to a knowledge. No hopes can be
entertained, that he will, at any time,
withdraw himself from the examination
either for Fellowships or Scholarships, even
if it were possible to convince him of the
ridiculous figure he makes on these occasions : for, as the statutes are framed, he
could not either vote, or nominate, at the
elections of Fellows or Scholars, if he ab-
sented

flourished most amongst the Greeks at the time of Alexander's
death ; but then his ignorance of Grecian history was such,
that he did not know but Alexander might have died during
the Peloponnesian war, and that consequently the candidate's
answer might be right. As the examination was publick, he
found it impossible to slur the matter, and was afraid to ex-
press either his approbation or disapprobation of the answer,
but remained some time in very laughable distress : at length
he determined to compound the affair, and to say something,
which wou'd neither fully admit, nor yet deny the propriety
of the answer, and stammered out, "Right, sir, but at
what time in that period?". The candidate still hesitating,
the Provost further stammered out, "Was it not at the
time of the death of Alexander?" The candidate then an-
swering yes ; the Provost expressed his applause with great
solemnity and pomp: Thus killing Alexander, in the time
of the Peloponnesian war, to manifest to the world his knowledge of Thucydides, that favourite author, whose name
he is so fond of repeating. *Risum Teneatis ?*

fented himfelf from the examinations which precede the filling up the refpective vacancies: and as the execution of his electioneering projects, in the College, is a more darling object with him, than even the gratification of his vanity, the College will never be freed from the difgrace, to which his attendance, on thefe occafions, muft expofe it, except by his removal or death. No remorfe, or fenfe of decency or fhame, will deter him from doing any thing whatfoever, which he thinks may conduce to his making a borough of the College, as will evidently appear from the detail of facts, fet forth in the remaining fheets of this publication. It has been urged, as a proof of his being a Scholar, that, when he was an undergraduate in the College, he had been accounted a promifing young man, and that fome premiums had been then adjudged to him, at the quarterly examinations, as rewards of his fuperior diligence and abilities: fuppofing this to be true, and giving it, as an argument in his favour, its full weight, it will not invalidate, in the leaft, any thing I have here advanced, refpecting his prefent ignorance of letters: almoft forty years have
elapfed,

elapfed, fince Mr. Hutchinfon quitted the
College: he ftaid only long enough to commence a Bachelor of Arts : the undergraduate courfe inftructs gentlemen barely
in the elements of the fciences ; fo tho'
it be admitted, that he was entitled to premiums, for his knowledge in the very firft rudi-
ment of learning, near forty years ago, it by no
means follows, either that he was then a perfon
of pregnant parts, or that he at prefent poffeffes any literary knowledge whatfoever; for
induftry, without much genius, may gain
to a man a little elementary knowledge,
which, if not improved, is very foon forgotten,
even in a fhorter time than forty years ;
and is, in itfelf, of very trifling confideration;
being but the cradle, the go-cart of fcience.
This argument, in favour of his learning,
puts me in mind of another doughty argument, in favour of his integrity, advanced
by an anonymous writer (probably himfelf)
that he cannot be a bad man, becaufe (as this
Writer afferts, whether truly, or otherwife,
I know not) he is a good hufband and father. To this it was oppofed, by an ingenious adverfary, that the fhepherd wou'd
hardly think the better of a Wolf, who
had

had overleaped the sheep-fold and devour-
ed the flock, becaufe it cou'd be proved,
that the beaft was kind to its mate and
cubs.

-·◈··◈·

Having thus finished the two firft parts
of my fubject, I fhall begin the third, to wit,
the account of Mr. Hutchinson's conduct in
the government of the College, with a
faithful tranflation of the oath of the Provoft, as contained in the third chapter of the
College ftatutes; only premifing, that the Provoft is obliged to take this oath kneeling,
in the College Chapel, before he enters on
the execution of his office, in the prefence of the whole body, and that Mr. Hutchinfon took it with that folemnity. This
oath is as follows:

" I ——, lately elected into the place
" of Provoft of the College of the Holy Tri-
" nity, fwear, that I will embrace the true
" religion of Chrift, from my very foul;
" that I will prefer the authority of fcrip-
" ture before the judgments of men; and
" that I will, from thence only, feek the
" rule for the regulation of my life, and the
" whole

" whole fum of my belief; that I will always
" hold the royal authority to be the fupreme
" in all things, and no way fubject to the
" jurifdiction of foreign bifhops ; and that I
" will always oppofe, to the beft of my pow-
" er and abilities, all opinions contrary to
" the true word of God. I alfo fwear, that
" I will preferve and adminifter all the bene-
" fices, funds, farms, poffeffions, royalties,
" rents, rights, liberties, privileges, and all
" the goods, in general, of the faid College,
" without diminution or wafte, as far as
" fhall lie in my power, and as by law I am
" able ; I will preferve the ftatutes of this
" College, to the utmoft of my power, in all
" things, *and I will give my affent to all*
" *things which fhall be done according to their*
" *prefcriptions* ; and I will govern and de-
" fend all and fingular the Fellows and
" Scholars, Penfioners, Sizers, and the other
" members of the College, by the fame
" laws and ftatutes, without refpect, favour,
" or hatred of, or to, any ftation, condi-
" tion or perfons ; and will take care, as
" far as in me lies, that all things aforefaid
" fhall be performed and defended lawfully
" and righteoufly by others : and alfo, that
" I will

" I will not, either upon my own bufinefs, or
" that of others, be abfent more than two
" months in the year from the College, unlefs
" either the affairs of the College, or nation,
" or the royal authority, fhall call me to fome
" other place ; or force, difeafe, peftilence,
" or fome other neceffary caufe of abfence
" fhall happen, to be approved of by the
" arch-bifhop of Dublin, in abfence of the
" chancellor. I alfo fwear, that if I fhall be
" removed from my place, or if I fhall, of my
" own accord, refign it, I will reftore all the
" goods of the College, in my power, to the
" Provoft, or treafurers of the College, im-
" mediately, if poffible, or within fifteen
" days, without controverfy or diminution.
" Laftly, I fwear, if I fhall be deprived of
" my office of Provoft, juftly and lawfully,
" that I will not, at any future time, bring
" any fuit or action, on that account, againft
" thofe who have lawfully deprived me :
" and alfo, that I will not afk, or procure,
" directly or indirectly, any difpenfation, con-
" trary to my oath, aforefaid, or contrary to
" the ordinances or ftatutes of the college,
" or any of them: thefe things, all and fingu-
" lar, I will obferve, fo help me God, ha-

G   " ving

" ving laid my hand on the Gofpels of
" Chrift."

Before I proceed further, I muft requeft,
that the reader will take fpecial notice of the
feveral claufes of this oath, and recur to it,
during the perufal of the remaining fheets ;
for, a due regard to brevity will not fuffer
me, always, to compare his actions, which
I am now about to relate, with the ftandard
of his oath. Such a comparifon may be a
matter of employment for the curiofity of
the reader. To give the publick a key to
the conduct of Mr. Hutchinfon, in the college, I muft remark, that there are two
grand objects, in the purfuit of which he
has been uniformly indefatigable, fince he
has been promoted to the place of Provoft :
his firft and moft darling object is to reduce
the College to a family borough, fo as always to have it in his power, to nominate
two of his fons, or dependants, it's reprefentatives in parliament. His eager purfuit
of this object has given occafion to moft un-
common exertions of his natural Fury, and
has been the immediate vifible caufe of his
moft outrageous and revengeful actions.
His

His fecond object is an ardent defire, as well from motives of vanity, as fecurity, to perfuade the nation in general, that he is a man of letters, and eminently qualified for the employment of Provoft. To his purfuit of this object muft be imputed, not only his ridiculous actions (many of which are of fuch a nature, as to excite the laughter and contempt only of the obfervers, without being very prejudicial to the College ; the detail of which I fhall therefore omit in general) but alfo actions of more ferious confequences, extremely ruinous to the learning and difcipline, which have hitherto flourifhed in the College, which, therefore I cannot, confiftently with my defign, omit to mention. He has another object, which he purfues with great affiduity, to wit, a defire of enriching himfelf, his family, and dependants, at the expenfe of the College funds ; but as this has not yet excited him to the commiffion of fuch flagrant enormities as the other two, as he has not yet had fufficient time, completely to execute his fchemes. I cannot, from incontrovertible facts, fo fully demonftrate it to be a fettled object with him, as each of the

G 2
othe̸ṛs

others is : however, fome facts I fhall mention in the following fheets, which leave very little room for doubt, that he has formed the moft ruinous fchemes of that kind, and that he will carry them into execution, if not in time prevented.

It is here proper to obferve, that, at the time of Mr. Hutchinfon's promotion to the Provoftfhip, two gentlemen were reprefentatives of the univerfity, in parliament, both of whom were recommended to the choice of the electors, by the late Provoft, who was always a faft friend to government, and that thefe gentlemen were, themfelves, its firm friends. One of them, as I have before mentioned, was then, and now is, his Majefty's Attorney-general in Ireland ; the other, a baronet of good reputation : A diffolution of parliament, from the operation of the octennial act, was to be expected in about two years after his promotion ; and he began his government of the College, by exerting all the powers of the Provoftfhip, to exclude the Attorney-general from reprefenting the College in the new parliament ; the other reprefentative declining any conteft
with

with him, his intereſt having expired with the late Provoſt. Thus, the very authority conferred on him by the crown was, in the firſt inſtance, exerted to exclude, from a feat in parliament, one of the firſt officers of the crown, and one of the ableſt and wiſeſt miniſters, which the King had ever employed in Ireland ; and from a feat which he had occupied, to the infinite benefit of the College, for thirty-nine years and upwards. His firſt exploit, in purſuance of this plan, was of an extraordinary nature, and turned out rather unluckily for him, his electioneering intereſt in the College not having received much benefit from it. About a year and a half before the diſſolution of the parliament, he ſent for ſuch of the Fellows as were tutors, whom he knew to have great intereſt with their pupils, and propoſed to them, as one object of their favour on the enſuing election, his eldeſt ſon ; told them he would ſoon ſelect, and propoſe to them, another perſon alſo, who ſhould be as well entitled to their favour as his ſon, and requeſted not only their votes and intereſt for his ſon, but that they would keep themſelves diſengaged from any promiſe to ſupport the intereſt of

G 3   any

any perfon, until fuch time as he fhould find
out another proper object for their choice.
This fon was the fame Eatonian, whom I
have already mentioned, who was not of
age, and whom he had juft then recalled
from Oxford, where, and at Eaton, he had
been educated, and entered him a Fellow-
commoner in this College, for the mere purpofe of fetting him up as a candidate for the
College, and procuring him fome acquain-
tance and intereft amongft the Students.
This propofal and addrefs was received
by fome with indignation ; by moft,
with coolnefs and referve : it feemed
ftrange to many of the Fellows, that
the Provoft fhould begin a canvafs, fo
long before even the probability of a vacancy, which, from the circumftances
of the College, and the difcontents which
reigned, on his then late promotion, muft
neceffarily throw the whole body into
a flame. They were amazed at the
prefumption of a man, who had been
newly, and extraordinarily, appointed Provoft, to the damage, and as it were in contempt, of the nation, and them, thus to
exprefs his expectation of being able to return

turn two perfons as reprefentatives of the
College, one a boy, with whofe education
he had not deigned to truft them; and the
other, a perfon whofe very name he had not
condefcended to impart to them. They
were no lefs furprifed, that he, who owed
all his promotions, nay almoft his *exiftence*,
to government, fhould omit, on fuch an occafion, to recommend to their choice their
old tried reprefentative, the King's Attorney
General, from whofe credit, and abilities,
the College had received the moft diftinguifhed favours, and effential fervices: but the
Provoft had his views in this hafty publication of his expectations; a regard to the
tranquillity of the College never entered his
mind; he was perfectly indifferent to the
dreadful effects of an electioneering flame,
lighted and blown up in a learned feminary,
fo long before the time of election : he cared
not if the whole body was confumed, provided he could carry his point, and fecure
the emoluments of his place, the only purpofes for which he had folicited the promotion : he intended to make ufe of the whole
exorbitant power of the Provoftfhip, to fecure the election of his candidates : if he
                                        fhould

fhould poftpone the declaration of his fentiments 'till the diffolution of parliament,
corruption would not have time to operate ;
the terrors he intended to difplay could have
but little weight with, the ruin he refolved
to bring but fmall effect on, the refractory,
before the election. The emoluments of
the College, natives places, exhibitions,
fcholarfhips, and even premiums, all heretofore facred, according to their primitive
deftination, to the nurture of the fciences,
formed the magazine, out of which the bafe,
venal, and illiterate, were to be furnifhed,
and arrayed, with the perverted rewards, and
ornaments, of the learned and ingenious.

The whole number of fcholarfhips, as I
have before obferved, amount to feventy;
fourteen or fifteen of thefe were to be diftributed on the examination for filling up vacant fcholarfhips, which was to happen before the election, and he determined that
no perfon fhould be elected a fcholar,
who would not previoufly promife to vote as
he fhould direct him ; he tampered with the
parents, friends, and connections of the
candidates, and found perfons bafe enough to
enter

enter into his views; in fact two only, out of
the whole number elected, had the honesty
and spirit to disappoint him. Time was required, as well for the filling up of this magazine, by the effluxion of the terms pre-
scribed by the statutes for the enjoyment of
Collegiate preferments, by death, cession, and
deprivation, as for the proper distribution
of its contents, for the actual purchasing of
votes, and for pointing out to all the members of the College the only path to academick benefits and honours, and thereby procuring votes by expectation, as well as by
actual enjoyment of emolument. In short,
the whole system of Collegiate rewards and
punishments was to be turned into one regular system of corruption and oppression, and
time was required as well for the operation,
as effect. Hence sprung the early publication of the Provost's designs, with respect
to the election of members of parliament.
When he had thus rung the alarm bell of a
canvass, the resentment of the College first
appeared, in an association of the scholars of
the house, encouraged by a few of the junior
Fellows. They determined to assemble, and
nominate two candidates, in opposition to
the

the one nominated, and the other to be nominated, by the Provoft. Thefe gentlemen
were convinced, that it would be in vain to
afk the ufe of either of the College-halls,
from the Provoft, to affemble in; and ftill
vainer to affemble in one of them without
his leave, as he would immediately difperfe
them : not one of their chambers was large
enough to contain their affembly, with
convenience; and there is a claufe in
the eleventh chapter of the ftatutes, forbidding their affembling in the College Courts;
which, tho' it was inferted merely to prevent
idlenefs and riot in the College, yet they all
knew the Provoft would make ufe of to
diffolve their affembly, if they fhould attempt, or if it had been practicable, to hold
it in the courts, or in any part of the College: they therefore determined to meet at
the principal tavern in the city of Dublin,
where they might have the advantage of a
large room to debate in, and where the Provoft had no ftatutable right to interrupt
them: and in purfuance of this defign, on
the ninth day of November, 1774, a notice
was affixed to the great gate of the hall, in
the

the following words: " The electors of the
" College are requested to meet this day, at
" two o'clock, at Ryan's, in Fownes's-street,
" to consider of proper persons to be put in
" nomination, as candidates for the Univer-
" fity." This was done, not so much with
a view of informing the electors of the time
and place of meeting, which were sufficiently
known, without the notice, as to let every
one see the purpose of their meeting, and to
obviate any artful mis-construction of it,
which the Provost might invent, to colour
any attempt of his to disperse them : having
taken this precaution, about forty of them
affembled at the time and place mentioned
in the notice.

The Provost, who had intelligence of
their intended meeting on the preceding day,
tho' he constantly attends the courts as a Barrister, from eleven o'clock in the morning
'till three in the evening, in Term time, and
during the Chancery fittings, left them, on
the day of the meeting, before two o'clock ;
hurried to the College, sent for the fenior
and junior Deans, both Clergymen and Fellows, and ordered them immediately to go
to

to Ryan's tavern, and command the scholars of the house, which they would find assembled there, instantly to disperse. The Deans went and delivered the Provost's orders; the scholars refused to obey; of which they immediately informed him : his turbulence and indecent behaviour on this occasion, can hardly be described; he ordered the Deans instantly to return and command them to disperse, with the denunciation of the severest penalties to the disobedient : he insulted and menaced the junior Dean, who at that time was the Rev. Mr. Richardson, (a gentleman whom he supposed not to have his interest much at heart) and behaved, in general, in such a manner, as strongly marked his perturbation : the Deans, however, returned to the assembly, which, on their second appearance, quietly dispersed. On the next day, he caused a board to meet; summoned a great number of the associating scholars to appear before it ; made several most tedious harangues, and endeavoured to persuade the board to agree to the inflicti-on of some academick punishment on two or three of the chiefs of the association ; but finding the majority averse from the

infliction

infliction of any punishment, his resentment
was at last obliged to abate of its expectations, and justly fearing that all his bustle and
fury in this affair would be turned into ridicule, if it should be found that the menac-
ing ebullitions of his rage, in the first pa-
roxysm of it, were utterly impotent, he at
length proposed, and even entreated, that
the board would agree to pass some censure
on the meeting. The majority, well knowing that any censure, they should pass on
the meeting, would by no means injure
any of the associators, willing, in some measure, by a trifling compliance, to indulge
the vanity of the man, to keep him if possible in temper, as nurses act to froward children, and contented to listen to the buzzing
of the wasp, when they had extracted the
sting, agreed that the scholars should be re-
primanded for their meeting, in a form prepared by the Provost, under the correction
of the board; which he pronounced in the
Board Room, to the associates, with his usual solemnity. Thus the catastrophe of this
mighty business was a farce, and, to heighten
the humour of it, the associators, during
their attendance on the board, in a parlour
of

of the Provoft's houfe, adjoining the room in
which the board was fitting, elected a chair-
man, propofed, nominated, and agreed to fupport two candidates on the enfuing election,
and all this they had full time to perform,
whilft the Provoft was difplaying his never-
ending oratory to the jaded, worn-out
board : thus executing, at a meeting fummoned by the Provoft himfelf, the very thing
which all his endeavours were levelled at
preventing. This unftatutable, illegal, and
arbitrary conduct of the Provoft, was immediately echoed thro' the city of Dublin, and
from thence thro' the nation. The electors
of the whole kingdom expreffed their indignation at the audacity of a man, who had
thus prefumed to violate the moft facred,
unalterable rights of electors, in manifeft
contempt of the laws and conftitution, and,
without having even the local ftatutes of the
particular corporation, whofe rights he had
invaded, to colour, much lefs to juftify, his
invafion. This conduct, fo far from promoting his electioneering intereft, ferved only
further to exafperate the electors of the College againft him, and cement their union.
Senfible at length of the illegality, as well as

imprudence

imprudence of the ſtep he had taken, he endeavoured, in ſome meaſure, to retrieve his
miſtake ; and, on the 28th day of November, 1774, a letter, addreſſed to the publick, ſigned Moderator, appeared in the Hibernian Journal, one of the daily papers,
in vindication of his proceedings on the occaſion. It is univerſally believed, has been
publickly aſſerted, and never was denied by
the Provoſt, or any of his partiſans, that
the letter was written by himſelf, and for
falſehood and miſrepreſentation it never
had its fellow. The ſubſtance of it is,
ſhortly, as follows ; the writer aſſerts, that
the head-porter of the College, about two
o'Clock, on the 19th of November, brought
the Provoſt the notice before-mentioned,
which he found poſted on the great gate of
the chapel : that the Provoſt, not entering
into the occaſion of this meeting, but conſidering the poſting of a notice in the College,
for the aſſembling of the ſcholars at a tavern,
as a dangerous innovation, deſtructive to
peace and diſcipline, ordered the aſſembly
to be diſperſed in the manner herein before-
mentioned ; that on the next day he con-
ſulted the Senior Fellows, and recommended

to them the moſt gentle mode of proceeding;
who agreed, that the ſcholars ſhould be re-
primanded : that there has been no example of ſuch a meeting, when there was no
vacancy, either in this or any other College :
that it was a great inſtance of the Provoſt's
lenity to refer this matter to the conſideration of the board ; he having a power to determine himſelf, in all matters relating to
diſcipline, which are not preciſely provided
for by the ſtatutes; and the writer, throughout, makes it his chief buſineſs, to exculpate the Provoſt from having, and actually
aſſerts that he had not, any electioneering
views in the tranſaction. The Provoſt, certainly, when he publiſhed this letter, imagined that neither of the Deans, nor any
member of the board, would publiſh the
truth of the tranſaction; but in this he was
miſerably deceived; for, very ſhortly after
its publication, an anſwer to it, ſigned *Verax*,
appeared in the ſame Journal, which effectually undeceived the publick, and to this he
never thought fit to reply. I was a member
of the board, ſummoned on this occaſion,
and very well remember the circumſtances
which then happened. He firſt informed us,

that

that he had received intelligence of an intended meeting of the scholars, on the 8th of November, the day before it was to be held; and also, that a notice of the time and place of meeting would be posted in the College on the 9th; that he had given orders to the head porter to watch for such a notice, to take it down, and bring it to him; and that he had determined to leave the courts early on the 9th, to disperse the meeting. Now, with respect to all these circumstances, Moderator is not only silent, but insinuates the contrary; for he would have us believe, that the first intelligence, which the Provost received of the meeting, was from the head porter, when he, as it were officially, brought him the notice at two o'clock on the 9th. To excuse the Provost's arbitrary behaviour in dispersing the assembly, the only thing he offers is, that the posting of a notice, for the meeting of the scholars at a tavern, was an innovation subversive of the College discipline. But every person, who knows the College for any length of time, can testify, that the posting of a notice in the College, for a meeting of the scholars at a tavern, to consider of the nomination of proper represen-

H   tatives,

tatives, is no innovation : it was done twice
before in my own memory, during the Provoſtſhip of the immediate predeceſſor of Mr.
Hutchinſon; it is a right inherent in the
electors to meet, on ſuch occaſions, when
and where they think proper ; the laws of
the land and conſtitution give it to them :
the ſtatutes of the College do not, nor could
they, take away this right from the electors
of the College. As for the flimſy pretence,
that the meeting of this aſſembly, in a tavern, was ſubverſive of diſcipline, it hardly
deſerves an anſwer : the meeting was before
dinner, when no intemperance was to be
feared ; the ſtatutes of the College do not
prohibit the Scholars from going to a tavern,
on ſuch a ſolemn occaſion, but only their
* frequenting taverns : the Provoſt well
knew the buſineſs they were upon ; the very notice proclaimed it ; it was a lawful
and a laudable buſineſs : but, ſays Moderator, there has been no inſtance of ſuch a
meeting of the electors of the College, before a vacancy ; in anſwer to this, it was
alleged, that no Provoſt, before Mr. Hutchinſon, had rendered ſuch a meeting neceſſary, before a vacancy : he began a
canvaſs,

* See the College Statutes, chap. 11.

canvafs, a year and a half before a vacancy,
with the views before-mentioned, and he
wifhed that his adverfaries had remained
quiet, until he had, by every unlawful method, which could be devifed, fecured the
election of his candidates, and rivetted the
chains of the college. The other inftance
of his lenity, the referring the matter to
the confideration of the board, is built on
an affertion, as falfe as any part of the letter ; to wit, that the Provoft may, in all
things refpecting difcipline, not exprefsly
provided for by the ftatutes, either determine
himfelf, or refer to the board : for the
fourth chapter of the ftatutes exprefsly pro-
vides, " *That the feven Senior Fellows fhall*
" *be, as it were, the Provoft's affeffors, and*
" *that he fhall tranfact all the greater*
" *affairs of the College, whether they refpect*
" *morals, learning, or œconomy, by their ad-*
" *vice or affiftance* :" the claufe in the fecond
chapter of the ftatutes, from which Moderator feems to have deduced this falfe pofition, no way warranting fuch an inference.
I hope I need not fay more to convince the
reader, that the Provoft had no other than
electioneering views in his difperfing the affembly, in the arbitrary, unwarrantable

H 2   manner

manner he did : and that all Moderator's affertions, to the contrary, are impudent
falfehoods : and I have been thus particular,
and prolix, in expofing the falfehoods contained in this firft publication, in behalf of
Mr. Hutchinfon, to give the reader fome idea
of the fhameful lengths, in untruth and mifreprefentation, fome perfons are capable of
going to, to ferve a turn, even when they
are liable to immediate detection.

The Provoft, finding by the ill fuccefs of
this, his firft, attack, on the independency
of the College, that he would meet with
more difficulty, than his vanity and folly had
before fuffered him to expect, in impofing
two of his creatures on the College, for reprefentatives, fet all the engines to work,
which the power of the Provoftfhip had given him the command of, with wonderful
affiduity, and without any regard whatfoever
to any confideration, inconfiftent with his
electioneering intereft. He met, indeed,
with a little interruption from one circumftance, which, as it brought infinite fcandal
and damage on the College, and is very expreffive of the man's temper and difpofition,
I fhall here relate, before I proceed further
with

with the detail of his operations in the College. His promotion to the Provoftfhip, fo exceffively injurious to the fociety, and to the whole nation, had given great offence to the kingdom in general, but was particularly galling to the members of the College: his infolence, turbulence, and pride, did not imprefs them with very favourable ideas of him; and his arbitrary, unwarrantable conduct, with refpect to the affociating fcholars, caufed thefe ill humours to burft forth: dread of the formidable power of the Provoftfhip had before fmothered them, but now refentment, fetting caution at defiance, fanned them to a blaze; the publick prints teemed with invectives, pafquinades, and accounts of his ignorance and brutality. This difaffection of the fcholars excited feveral gentlemen to take advantage of it, and to offer themfelves candidates for the honour of reprefenting the College in parliament, on the expected election; amongft thefe was one Mr. Doyle, who publifhed his pretenfions in a printed hand-bill, addreffed to the electors of the College: this addrefs was fhort, and feemed to be written in a great hurry, as it was but indifferently penned; it contained no abufe of the Provoft, and could do

him

him no mifchief, the writer's intereft in the
College being very feeble : but the wrath
of a fool is foon kindled ; it touched a fore
part ; the very idea of an oppofition, on an
election, fet the Provoft in a flame, tho' he
was incapable of judging, whether the addrefs was well or ill penned ; whether it
could injure him or not ; yet it was a publick avowal of a man's intention to oppofe
his intereft in the College on an election, and
this, to him, was a deadly affront.—In the
firft emotions of his rage, he had fome
thoughts of challenging Mr. Doyle to fingle
combat ; thefe were immediately ftifled by
certain prudent apprehenfions, concerning his
perfonal fafety : he found himfelf in pretty
much the fame fituation with *Cacofogo* in
the play, when he exclaims, " Now, were I
valiant, wou'd I flay him : he took fome
time to inquire into the character and fituation of Mr. Doyle, and happily found that
he had been for fome time confined to his
room, and often to his bed, by a violent
diforder, which almoft deprived him of the
ufe of both his eyes and limbs : this account
of Mr. Doyle's fituation renewed his ardour
for battle ; but ftill he judged it the moft'
prudent way to fight by proxy, probably
                                            thinking

thinking his fkill in law might be queftioned, if he fought in perfon, when every lawyer knew that the parties, in a writ of right, may fight by champions; or, perhaps, being as circumfpect as Falftaff, who was afraid that the dead man might be a counterfeit as well as himfelf, and the better counterfeit of the two; for thefe reafons, or fome others equally powerful, he declined challenging Mr. Doyle himfelf, and refigned that province to his fon, the candidate for the College; and Mr. Doyle, being unable to ftand without a crutch, or fee at two yards diftance, as the Provoft very well knew, was obliged to decline the combat, until fuch time as he fhould fo far recover the ufe of his legs and eyes, as to be able to ftand and fee. Whilft this affair of honour, between Mr. Doyle and his fon, lay over, one of the parties having been bound to keep the peace, and the performance of the duel being thus adjourned to another day and kingdom, the Provoft became a little too free in his difcourfe refpecting Mr. Doyle, and declared in many companies that he would chaftife him, when his fon had done with him, if he furvived the dreadful encounter; thinking there was but little danger to be apprehended

hended from a man who had already a quar-
rel on his hands, which bodily infirmity
prevented him from terminating. Mr. Doyle,
beginning to recover, tho' flowly, and being informed of thefe vaunts, fent a gentleman one morning to the Provoft, to let him
know that he was fo far recovered, as
to be able to give him an opportunity of attempting the execution of his menaces, at
a certain hour and place. This meffage fomewhat difconcerted the Provoft: all the reputation in arms he pretended to, lay at ftake;
he could not, confiftently with the character
of a modern man of honour, which he had
affumed, reject the propofal; pofting ftared
him in the face; he agreed, at length, to meet
his antagonift, determined to take a peace-
officer with him, as a fecond; but procuring certain intelligence, before the time appointed for the meeting, that Mr. Doyle
was yet fo feeble as to be fcarce able to ftand
without affiftance, and that his eye-fight
was fo weak as to prevent his feeing at the
diftance of ten yards, he rallied his fcattered
fpirits, and took the refolution of meeting,
without fraud or guile, his lame and blind
antagonift. They met, fired a piftol each,
and made up the matter without blood; Mr.
Doyle

Doyle being fo infirm, that he could not
venture to ftand on the grafs, in the field of
battle, for fear of cold, but was obliged to
take his poft on a gentleman's coat, fpread
out for the purpofe. Any reafonable perfon
would imagine, if a man in the Provoft's
ftation was unfortunate enough, through
folly and paffion, to illaqueate himfelf in a
duel, and had acquitted himfelf in it with
fpirit and honour, that decency, prudence,
and even attachment to his own intereft,
would induce him to endeavour, as much
as poffible, to keep it a profound fecret: but
to the arguments of prudence and decency
Mr. Hutchinfon never liftened, nor was he
qualified to underftand their force: and he
was fo far from thinking the character of a
duellift injurious to his intereft, that the †
acquifition of it was the very fummit of his
ambition,

† He has confirmed the juftice of this remark, by feveral
inftances of his conduct, fince his affair with Mr. Doyle; he
publickly read to moft of the Fellows of the College, with
the higheft marks of triumph and fatisfaction, a letter which
he had received from a gentleman, giving an account of his
fon's behaviour, in a duel with Mr. Doyle, ftyling him his
gallant fon; this fon was, at the fame time, a member of the
College, and liable to expulfion for fighting a duel, by the
College ftatutes. The gentlemen, to whom he read the letter,
were the Governors of the College, and Clergymen. An information

ambtion, the only method in his opinion of eftablifhing his throne in the College. His petulance had before hurried him into fome quarrels, out of which he had made but a fcurvy retreat : tho' one of his former antagonifts had been a cripple.* He thought Mr. Doyle's fituation gave him a fair opportunity of retrieving his reputation in arms, and that his adverfaries would hereafter dread the refentment of an hero, fo renowned in war. A pompous account of this holiday duel was immediately publifhed in moft of the News-papers in England and Ireland, and the magnanimity of the Provoft, on the occafion, extolled to the fkies. The glory of Wolfe was not celebrated in more exalted ftrains ; and, to heighten the abfurdity of this

formation has been granted againft the Provoft himfelf lately, by the unanimous opinion of the Judges of the King's Bench, for challenging the Attorney-General, a gentleman between 70 and 80 years old, in the hall of the courts. This challenge to the Attorney-General has demonftrated his pufillanimity to the world; for he challenged this old gentleman, well knowing that his age, ftation and dignity, precluded even the poffibility of a duel; and challenged him too, without any provocation, and merely to glofs over his own want of fpirit, in declining a combat with a gentleman, fully his equal, whom he had ill-treated, and who had publickly chaftifed him for it.

* The late Dr. Lucas.

this proceeding, it was manifeſt to every one acquainted with the Provoſt's manner of writing (which his frequent publications, about this time, made ſufficiently known) that he himſelf had drawn up this account. This behaviour was attended with very miſchievous effects to the College. Our nation is, perhaps too juſtly, reproached with a propenſity to duelling, ariſing either from natural warmth of temper, or an erroneous education, or both. Our Engliſh neighbours are confeſſedly as brave a nation as any in Europe, and yet are not near ſo much addicted to this murderous vice : What then muſt be the opinion of every ſober man in the kingdom, of this conduct of the Provoſt ? he is placed at the head of a ſeminary, inſtituted for the education of all the youth in the kingdom, deſigned for learned profeſſions, but chiefly for the ſervice of the church; the youthful fire of his pupils can hardly be confined, within proper limits, by the ſteady conduct of wiſe and good men, with the powerful aſſiſtance of moſt rigorous ſtatutes : what then muſt be the dreadful conſequences of this fire, not only ſuffered to rage *uncontroled*, but even blown up and ſupplied with combuſtibles, by the very perſon,

son, whofe duty it is to exert all his endeavours for its extinction? unhappy Ireland!
whofe infant children are thus, as it were,
educated to mutual flaughter, their native
vices carefully cherifhed to malignant maturity! unhappy church! whofe growing fons
are nurtured in the principles of revenge and
murder! and exemplarily taught to deride
the peaceful precepts of their meek redeemer.
Will fuch inftitutions produce painful minifters of the gofpel, who by their preaching
will perfuade, by their examples excite men
to the exercife of all the chriftian virtues?
Will men, thus educated, practife the patience, forbearance and humility, enjoined to
his difciples, by our bleffed Saviour, when
he orders them, if fmitten on one cheek, to
turn the other alfo? Alas! it is not to be expected; human paffions are too powerful to be
fubdued, when not only fuffered to grow
unmolefted in the youthful breaft, but when
their growth is encouraged by the example
of our mafters and teachers : they are then
ftrengthened and confirmed by authority and
habit, and become, as it were, a part of our
nature. This wicked conduct, in the head
of a learned Seminary, would not be endured
even in the mafter of the military fchool of
cadets

cadets at Greenwich ; the very commanders
of armies difcountenance the practice of duelling amongft their officers ; how deteftable
then is the conduct of this man, who has
thus poifoned, by his pernicious example, the
very fountain, which hitherto diffufed the
healing waters of eternal life throughout the
nation ! the effects are already vifible ; fcarce
a week paffes, without a duel between fome
of the ftudents ; fome of them have been flain';
others maimed ; the College-park is publickly made the place for learning the exercife of
the piftol ; fhooting at marks, by the gownfmen, is every day's practice ; the very chambers of the College frequently refound with
the explofions of piftols ; the Provoft has introduced a fencing-mafter into the College,
and affigned him the Convocation, or Senate-
houfe of the Univerfity, for a fchool, to teach
the gownfmen the ufe of the fword ; tho'
the ufe of fwords is ftrictly forbidden in the
College, by the ftatutes, and tho' fuch ftudents, as chufe to learn the art of fencing,
may readily procure inftruction in the city.
A ftudent complained to the board that he
had been challenged by another gownfman
to fight with piftols ; the Provoft would not
fuffer the board to take any cognizance of

the

the affair ; the perfon complained of, being then one of the gang, he has openly muf-
tered in the College, for the purpofes I fhall
hereafter relate, and perhaps he alfo thought
that clergymen were not proper judges of the
point of honour : fo that this conduct has convinced the ftudents, as much as if he had publickly proclaimed it, that fwords, or piftols,
are the only arbiters of their difputes, which
he approves of, or which he will permit ;
and the College is likely to become a fcene
of general carnage and confufion.

After this attack, on the affociating fcholars before-mentioned, he became indefatigable in exerting all the means, right and
wrong, which he could procure or devife for
the purpofe of fecuring the election of his
candidates. Two powers are vefted in the
Provoft, by the ftatutes, which he made a
very bad ufe of, and rendered very fervice-
able to his defign ; the one, the power of
granting leave of abfence from the College
to the Fellows and Scholars, ; the other,
that of interfering, in a limited manner, in the
diftribution of chambers, which, by various
arts, as I fhall hereafter fhew, he fwelled into an unlimited power of difpofing of them,
to fuch perfons as he thought proper. By
the

the twenty-fecond chapter of the ftatutes, it
is provided, " That each of the Fellows and
" Scholars, when they have any neceffary
" caufe of abfenting themfelves, fhall afk
" the Provoft, or, in his abfence, the Vice-
" Provoft, leave of abfence, and fhall write
" his name, and the day on which he leaves
" the College, in a regifter, to be kept by
" the Provoft, or, in his abfence, by the Vice-
" Provoft, and fhall alfo write the day of his
" return in the fame regifter, on the very
" day of his return, or the day after : and
" that if any of the Fellows, or Scholars,
" fhould, either thro' negligence, or on pur-
" pofe, omit the performance of thefe re-
" quifites, he fhould, for the firft omiffion,
" be mulcted one week's commons ; for the
" fecond omiffion, two week's commons; for
" the third, three ; and for the fourth omif-
" fion, be punifhed, according to the dif-
" cretion of the Provoft, and the majority
" of the fenior Fellows." It is, by the fame
chapter, further provided, " That every
" Fellow fhall be allowed fixty-three days
" of abfence, in a year ; and every Scholar
" thirty-two; to be computed from Trinity
" Sunday annually : and that if they do not
" return within thefe times refpectively, they
" fhall be expelled, unlefs they obtain leave
" of

" of longer abfence from the Provoſt (or,
" in his abfence, from the Vice-Provoſt)
" and the majority of the Board, for ſome
" ſufficient reafon, which reafon (if leave has
" been obtained in the Provoſt's abfence)
" is to be approved of by him, when he re-
" turns to the College." This ſtatute, the
reader muſt obferve, is very ſtrict, and penal,
and tho' it is not part of my prefent bufinefs
to inquire, whether ſuch rigour was neceſſary, or not, at the time of penning the ſtatutes, yet it may not be entirely ufelefs to
obferve, that conſtant refidence in the College might have then been more neceſſary,
than at prefent; for the great object of the
inſtitution, as I often before obferved, was
to wean the natives of Ireland from the er-
rors of Popery, to which they were wedded
with extraordinary, and almoſt univerfal attachment, both at the time of the foundation of this College, and of the penning
the new ſtatutes : it was therefore a wife provifion, that the Students, (numbers of whom,
at that time, were either defcended from
Popiſh parents, or had near relations of that
perfuafion) ſhould have as little intercourfe as
poſſible with them, until they had been ſufficiently confirmed in the principles of the
true Proteſtant faith, by a long refidence and
ſtudy

ſtudy in the college. The neceſſity of a conſtant reſidence of the ſcholars induced a neceſſity that the Fellows alſo, or, at leaſt, a conſiderable number of them, ſhould be conſtantly reſident. But the times are now greatly changed : knowledge is now diffuſed almoſt univerſally : many of the moſt pernicious ſuperſtitions of Popery are now repudiated by the very followers of that ſect : the true light of the goſpel has ſhot its rays into the obſcureſt corners of this kingdom : a great majority of the ſtudents are, and have been, for at leaſt half a century paſt, of old Proteſtant families : hence conſtant reſidence, either of the Fellows or Scholars, in the College, throughout the year, is not now ſo neceſſary as heretofore ; nay, ſuch reſidence would be even pernicious, as well to the health as morals of the ſtudents, on account of the ſurprizing increaſe of the city of Dublin, which, in the reign of Charles the Firſt, had not arrived to the tenth part of its preſent magnitude. The College, which was then ſituated near half a mile from the city, and ſurrounded by parks and gardens, is now encloſed within it : the vices of great cities increaſe with their bulk, and as the

I   College

College terms, when the students are in-
structed by the publick professors, and their
tutors, do not last above six months in the
year, the Fellows and Scholars, if obliged,
during vacations, to keep constant residence,
would be greatly injured. Vacations would
furnish the scholars with opportunities of indulging their youthful propensity to pleasure,
amidst the dissipation of a metropolis, to the
ruin of their health and morals; and the
health of both Fellows and Scholars would
be impaired, by breathing constantly the
corrupted † air of a great city. For these
reasons the rigour of this statute was greatly
relaxed: it was one of these laws, which, in
course of time, repeal themselves. Before the
promotion of the present Provost, it was,
during vacations, particularly the long Au-
tumnal vacation, never, or at least very seldom, put in force : it could answer no purpose, but an electioneering one, to enforce
obedience to it, in the long vacation; as all
College business is then at a stand, and even
the

† Doctor Percival, of Manchester, has proved, by long
and accurate observations, that the ratio of deaths annually,
even in the comparatively small town of Manchester, is to
that of deaths in the adjacent country, as two to one. How
greatly must this ratio be increased in such a city as Dublin?

the doors of the chapel clofed for fix weeks
together. The power, however, given to
the Provoft, by this ftatute, Mr. Hutchinfon greedily laid hold of, to further his defigns; and, tho' the law was in a manner an-
tiquated and in itfelf pernicious, not only
revived it in it's fulleft extent, but ftretched
it infinitely beyond its bounds, for the oppreffion of all, who would not promife to
vote on the enfuing election, as he fhould
direct them. To the fame righteous ufe,
indeed, he applied every penal claufe in the
whole code of ftatutes; purpofing (as one of
his partifans, a reverend Divine, openly declared) to make fuch of the members, as
fhould prefume to oppofe his intereft, wifh
themfelves rather in Hell, than in the College; whilft to fuch Fellows and Scholars, as
favoured his intereft, he gave the moft ample
indemnity, not only with refpect to the ftatute of abfence, but all the other ftatutes
whatfoever. This ftatute of abfence was
one of the moft powerful electioneering engines: for the fcholars of the houfe are the
only voters in the College, except the Fellows; and as, by the 5th chapter of the ftatutes, no perfon can be elected a fcholar, who

has

has an annual income of twenty pounds,
either in poffeffion or expectancy, and as
poverty is exprefsly made one of the qualifications for a fcholarfhip,—they are generally perfons of narrow circumftances, whofe
prefent fubfiftence, and future provifion in
life, depend, in a great meafure, on the emoluments they derive from their literary acquirements : hence many of them are obliged
to become under-teachers in great fchools,
and private tutors in gentlemen's families in
the country, and cannot therefore be conftantly refident, according to the prefcriptions of the ftatute : and their abfence, on
fuch occafions, had been generally connived
at, before Mr. Hutchinfon's promotion to
the Provoftfhip. By his exacting a ftrict con-
formity to this ftatute, from all who would
not promife to vote at the election, as he
was pleafed to dictate, and giving a general
indemnity, from the penalties of it, to every
one who promifed to comply with his de-
fires, he, from the operation of this ftatute
alone, procured a great proportion of the
feventy fcholars to vote as he thought proper. I fhall give examples of his conduct,
in this refpect, when I come to treat of his
behaviour

behaviour to individuals; and hope the reader will remember the direction I formerly
hinted to him, to recur frequently to the Provoſt's oath, before recited, and that he will, on
this occaſion particularly, compare his conduct, in reſpect to the ſtatute of abſence,
which I have ſtated truly and impartially,
with that clauſe of his oath, which relates
to his government of the members of the
College.

His management in the diſtribution of
chambers comes next to be conſidered. In
the 21ſt chapter of the ſtatutes is a clauſe,
of which the following is a tranſlation.
" In the diſtribution of chambers, altho'
" an attention ought to be paid to the learn-
" ing and virtue of ſuch as apply for them,
" yet, left, from ſuch attention, contro-
" verſy and envy ſhould ariſe, we ordain,
" *that the Senior ſhall be always preferred*
" *to the Junior, as well amongſt the Fellows*
" *as Scholars*, unleſs the Provoſt ſhould, *per-*
" *haps* judge *for ſome important cauſe*
" that ſuch ſucceſſion ſhould be *ſometimes*
" changed. But this diſcretionary power
" he is to exerciſe amongſt the Scholars only.
" And

" And it is our pleasure, that this power,
" of diftributing chambers, fhould be exer-
" cifed by the Provoft alone, and that no
" perfon fhall enjoy a chamber as his own,
" unlefs he is firft admitted to the poffeffion
" of it by the Provoft : and therefore, when
" the Provoft is abfent, or the Provoftfhip
" vacant, nothing in this matter fhall be
" attempted." Thus we find a very limited
power, with refpect to the diftribution of
the chambers, is vefted in the Provoft : the
line of his conduct is chalked out ; the fenior claimant is always to be preferred : and
this he muft always follow, unlefs fome very important reafon fhould induce him to deviate from it. That part of the claufe,
which gives to the Provoft alone the power,
of diftributing chambers, is only inferted, to
prevent the Vice-Provoft, and Board, from
interfering in the diftribution, as appears by
the fubfequent part of the claufe ; and does
not any way change or alter the obligation
laid on the Provoft, to diftribute the chambers according to feniority. This limited
power he, by various ftratagems and arts,
turned into an abfolute power, of diftributing chambers to his creatures only, accord-

ing

ing to his will and pleasure : and what benefit his electioneering interest has received, by
the operation of this engine, will appear
from a consideration of the present state of
the chambers. The buildings of the College are not large enough to accommodate
more than one half of the Students with
lodgings ; on this account every vacant chamber is sought after by a number of compe-
titors : gentlemen, resident in the country,
do not care to trust such of their children,
as they design for the College, to live at large
in a great city, and therefore make use of
all their interest to procure the favour of the
Provost, in hopes that their children will
be soon accommodated with apartments in
the College : from the same reason they are
inclined to place their children under such
tutors only, as they believe to be favourites
with the Provost : and Mr. Hutchinson,
knowing that the tutors have great influence
over their pupils, took pains to encourage
this inclination in parents, by making use
of all his arts (for, as I before observed, he
is not deficient in low-cunning) to prevent
the pupils of any of the fellows, except
such as are devoted to his interest, from obtaining

taining chambers. A custom had been established, before his promotion, of advertising the vacancy of each chamber, on the College gate, for a week previous to the granting it to a new possessor, and of assembling all the tutors weekly, and reading over the list of vacant chambers, at which time each tutor mentioned such of his pupils as wanted chambers, and their pretensions in point of seniority. It had been usual, at these assemblies, at least in the time of the late Provost, to give a preference to a Fellow-commoner before a pensioner, altho' the pensioner was senior ; the late Provost thinking, that the encouragement of young gentlemen of large fortunes, to repair to this College for their education, by indulging them in some privileges, was, as being serviceable to the nation in general, a cause, sufficiently important, to warrant his deviation from the rule, respecting seniority. Mr. Hutchinson has, at times, waved these customs, and at times observed them, as best suited his views. Vacant chambers have been sometimes assigned by him to particular persons, without their having been previously advertised, or

the

the tutors knowing any thing of the matter;
by which means they have been cut off
from the opportunity of stating the statutable claims of their respective pupils
to such chambers: at other times, and
very frequently, he has postponed the af-
sembling of the tutors for three weeks together, and then has given notice, at seven or
eight o'clock in the morning, in winter, for
their immediate meeting, when he well
knew, that some of the most eminent of
them, who are married men, and reside with
their families in the city, were absent from
the College, and thus, the claims of the pupils
of the absentees could not be mentioned.
The rule, respecting the preference to Fel-
low-commoners, observed by the late Provost, he turned very dexterously to the service of his designs. He counted, pretty justly,
only two of the tutors staunch to his interest: when one of these staunch gentlemen
made a claim to a vacant chamber, on behalf of a pupil, who happened to be a Fellow-commoner, and a claim was made by
another tutor, to the same chamber, in behalf of his pupil, who happened to be a pensioner, and with the advantage of seniority
over the other claimant, he immediately adjudged the chamber to the Fellow-commoner,
declaring,

declaring, that he would not break thro' eftablifhed cuftoms : but when the Fellow-commoner claimant was the pupil of any tutor,
except of thefe two ftaunch gentlemen, and
the oppofite claimant pupil to one of them,
and a penfioner, with feniority on his fide ;
he immediately decided in favour of the penfioner, declaring, that feniority was the
rule prefcribed for his conduct by the ftatutes. Thus, *quaque via*, the poffeffion of
the chamber was adjudged to the pupil of
his favourite.

In this College, the Junior Fellows are
but flenderly provided for : the annual income of their Fellowfhips is but £40, fo that
their chief fupport arifes from the pupils ;
and the Senior Fellows have left the pupilage totally in their hands, from a confideration of the fcanty maintenance allotted to
them ; each penfioner pays his tutor annually £6, each Fellow-commoner £12 : any
attempt, therefore, of the Provoft, to dimi-
nifh the number of one Fellow's pupils, and
increafe the number of another's, is moft fig-
nal injuftice. From the exorbitant power vefted in the Provoft, it cannot be eafily imagined, what advantage, in point of pupils,
a Fellow

a Fellow derives from the Provoſt's countenance ; but when the ſtatutes are perverted
to increaſe the income of one or two, by
the oppreſſion and ruin of the reſt, the tyranny is inſupportable : and what effects his
flagrant partiality, in diſtribution of chambers, has had on the pupilage of his favourites, and of thoſe he is pleaſed to diſtinguiſh
by the name of his enemies, are too obvious
and lamentable to eſcape the obſervation of
every member of the College. By theſe
means, and others, equally juſt, he ſtill endeavours to throw the whole pupilage of the
College into the hands of a few men, who
have ſerved, and promiſed for the future to
ſerve, his electioneering intereſt ; with the
view, as well of ſecuring their votes and
influence with their pupils, as of manifeſt-
ing, to the other Fellows, his determination to ſtop at nothing, which may tend to
their utter ruin, unleſs they give themſelves
up, as it were, body and ſoul, to his ſervice. Beſides the benefits which he has already derived, and expects to derive, from
the Fellows, by his diſtribution of chambers,
he procured ſome votes, on the laſt election,
by his own immediate traffick, in the ſame
way,

way, with the fcholars, without the inter-
vention of the Fellows. On the death of the
late Mr. Shewbridge, who was one of the
Junior Fellows, he granted his chambers, in
joint-tenancy, to a fcholar of the houfe and
a private pupil, with whofe education the
fcholar was intrufted, but who was not any
member of the College. His granting chambers in the College, to a perfon who was not
a member of the College, was animadverted
upon in a * publication, ftating part of his
conduct, which made its appearance about
half a year after he had granted them.
This publication, from the fpirit with which
it was written, and the truths it contained,
alarmed him : the material charges could
not be denied : but as a drowning man will
catch at a twig, he felected two or three of
the moft trivial accufations it contained,
which he commiffioned his emiffaries either
to deny or extenuate. This charge of granting chambers to a perfon, who was not a
member of the College, he attempted to re-
fute in a very ridiculous manner. The
grant was inferted in the regiftry of chambers : at the time of its infertion, the Rev.
Dr. Dabzack, a gentleman, who (as will
appear in the following fheets) had entirely
devoted

* Preface to the Appendix Pranceriana.

devoted himfelf to his fervice, was regifter
of chambers ; but unluckily for the Provoft,
at the time of the publication, the Rev. Mr.
Drought was regifter, and in poffeffion of
the regiftry : he had no hopes that Mr.
Drought would obliterate the entry at his requeft, and certify that no fuch entry had
been made ; he was a man of integrity, had
never fhewn much inclination to his fervice,
and had dangerous connections. What was
to be done ? he was determined to deny the
fact : but the entry in the regiftry was a formidable bar. After much deliberation, he affembled the board ; the regiftry was produced ; the obnoxious entry read, the Provoft
folemnly afferted, that he had granted the
chambers to the Scholar alone, and not to his
pupil, and Dr. Dabzack humbly confeffed,
(as was concerted) that the pupil's name was
inferted by his miftake; and then the Provoft
ordered the pupil's name to be obliterated. I
was then a member of the board, and do not
ever recollect to have been in greater diftrefs, than by fuppreffing a violent inclination to laugh at this farce, which was acted
with great folemnity; particularly as the
Provoft confeffed, that this pupil of the fcho-

lar

lar was the fon of a man, whom he had particular reafons to oblige, and that he had really granted the chambers to the Scholar for his pupil's ufe, when he fhould be qualified to enter the College. But this ingenuity of the Provoft was not attended with the effects he expected : by his endeavours to exculpate, he only expofed himfelf more to the arrows of juft reprehenfion : for this Scholar of the houfe had been a Sizer, and it was well known he was unable to purchafe fuch chambers ; fo that every one was convinced that they were really purchafed by the pupil, and were his property : befides, thefe chambers were very large, having been the lodgings of a Fellow, and contained room fufficient for the convenient lodging of five fcholars : fo that the Provoft, by granting them all to one perfon, deprived four fcholars of habitations, of which, as I before mentioned, there was a great fcarcity. But he fecured the Scholar's vote by it ; and fimilar motives had already excited him to commit actions infinitely more detrimental to the College.

The place of regifter of chambers is elective

tive annually : it is always beftowed on a
Junior Fellow; and as it is generally efteemed
the beft employment to which a Junior Fellow is entitled : the Senior amongft the Junior Fellows had a fort of prefcriptive right
to it. On that vacancy of this place, which
immediately preceded the laft election of
members of parliament, I was Senior of the
Junior Fellows ; and the Provoft would by
no means confent, that I fhould be elected
into the place: he had, by that time, been fully convinced, that I was not a man who
would concur in any of his fchemes of ambition or deftruction ; and fufpected that I
was one of thofe perfons, who daily expofed
his conduct in the publick prints: he apprehended therefore, if I was Regifter of chambers, that his management, in the diftribution of them, would be revealed to the world.
The majority of the board, of which I was
then a member, would not agree to elect
any other perfon, in prejudice to my prefcriptive right ; and he had, in this cafe, no power of nomination : to extricate himfelf from
this difficulty, he propofed an augmenta-
tion to the falary of another place, by the
addition of £20 annually, fo as to make it
equal

equal in profit to the place of regifter of chambers, and to agree to my election into that place. I did not approve of this method of augmenting the falaries of places, out of the College-revenues, to promote the Provoft's jobs, but when I confidered that the blame could not lie at my door, but at his, who thus prevented me from enjoying a place to which I was entitled ; and that the emoluments of the place, with the increafed falary, were only equal to that of the place which was unjuftly witheld from me, I agreed to accept of his propofal and afterwards affifted, by my vote, in the election of a very particular friend into the place of regifter of chambers, to his great mortification.

In refpect to the diftribution of College-emoluments amongft the fcholars, he acted almoft without difguife, but the better to know what perfons were proper objects to work upon, he introduced an electioneering agent into the College, and affigned him large and commodious chambers. This man, to the great fcandal of his profeffion, is in holy orders, and employed himfelf in corrupting and debauching the Scholars of the houfe ;

houfe ; his chambers were the court of Comus; all manner of revelry went forward in them with great fpirit : he hunted the Scholars from the hall, and chapel, to their chambers ; attacked them 'in the courts ; enticed them to partake of his good cheer, and, when he had conciliated their favour by bumpers, allured them into his nets by the baits of College preferment ; no ftudent could procure any favour but thro' his mediation: in fhort he was the Blacquiere of Mr. Hutchinfon : but as this Rev. Gentleman's conduct is fhortly to be reviewed by a proper tribunal, I fhall wave any further mention of him.

At the firft election of the fcholars, after Mr. Hutchinfon's promotion, he acted, indeed, with fome addrefs : he perfectly knew the inclinations and connections of all the candidates, from his electioneering agent and his fpies, who found means to introduce themfelves into every company in the College. Such candidates, as, by themfelves or their friends, had made their terms with his agent, or himfelf, were recommended to his friends at the Board ; fo that they were fure of having four fuffrages amongft the electors, who amounted but to eight, and they had an equal chance with the other candi-

dates

dates of meriting the suffrages of the remaining four; the other candidates had four
certain votes against them, and only such
chances, as their merits gave them, of obtaining the votes of the other four; hence
the chances became so great, in favour of
the Candidates approved of by the Provost,
that all he had selected obtained scholarships,
except two; for of the whole number then
elected, being fifteen, two only, as I before
observed, voted on the election of members
of parliament contrary to his interest. This
election of scholars was managed in pretty
much the same manner with the election of
the sixteen Peers of Scotland, where such
Peers are generally elected as are inserted
in the Minister's recommendatory list, sent
to the electors, previous to the election.
At the last election of scholars of the house
he could not attend; as his own election at
Corke commenced about the same time: neither was his attendance so necessary, as on
the former occasion; as it happened subsequent to the election of members of parliament, and therefore the scholars then elected
could not hurt his interest, as their scholarships would probably expire before the next
election of members. I was, on this occasion, one of the seven electors, (the Provost's
            absence .

abfence having reduced them to that number) and could not help obferving the conduct of his principal Minifter at the Board, the Rev. Doctor Leland :* this Doctor Leland is the next Senior Fellow to the Vice-Provoft, who is firft in point of feniority, and the vote of each elector is collected in order, beginning with the fenior : in two or three inftances, when it came to Doctor Leland's turn to vote, he declared he was in doubt whether he fhould give his beft mark, † or not, to the candidate, and requefted to hear the opinions of other gentlemen, and I took notice that he always gave his good and bad mark, in direct oppofition to the marks given by two or three other gentlemen, one of whom I was, who were well known to be no favourers of the Provoft's jobs. This conduct was too palpable to efcape reprehenfion. It feemed ftrange, that a man, folemnly fworn to act impartially, fhould withhold his opinion of a candidate's merit, under a pretence of being in doubt, until fuch time as he had heard the opinions of the other gentlemen

K 2 concerning

---

* The reader is defired not to miftake this gentleman for the learned Doctor Leland of Dublin, author of the Review of Deiftical Writers, and many other tracts.

† A technical expreffion relating to the manner of voting for fcholars in the College.

concerning it, and fhould then form an opinion diametrically oppofite to theirs : I at laft
rofe, and told the Vice-Provoft, that I
would not vote, 'till Doctor Leland had given his vote abfolutely, in his order ; on
which that Doctor openly propofed that the
order of voting fhould be inverted, and that
the junior fhould vote firft, by which means
he would become the laft voter but one, and
be able to form a clearer judgment how he
could beft difpofe of his vote for the fervice
of his patron : this was over-ruled unanimoufly : the job was too evident to be fupported even by the Provoft's friends ; and,
during the remainder of the election, the
Doctor was obliged to rely on his own information and fagacity, in difpofing of his
votes, the Provoft not being in Dublin to
give him inftructions. This conduct of Doctor Leland would induce one to think, that
he fufpected fuch gentlemen, as refifted the
arbitrary meafures of the Provoft, had forgotten the folemn obligation laid on them by
the oath taken by every elector, who is obliged to fwear, that, laying afide favour or
hatred, he will elect only fuch, as feem to him
beft qualified according to the ftatutes, and
that therefore, he thought the moft effectual
method he could take, of ferving his patron's
interest,

intereft, was to vote in direct oppofition to
them; without at all confidering the merit
of the candidate, as he was by his oath
bound to do. If fuch were the motives of
his conduct, I leave it to the impartial publick to judge, whether fuch thoughts are har-
boured in the breafts of the uncorrupt and
ingenuous. It is further to be obferved, that
Doctor Leland exerted this ingenuity, at a
time when the fcholars, to be elected, had
only a probable chance, by the death of one
of the members in parliament for the College, of ever voting at an election, the
term prefcribed by the ftatutes, for the enjoyment of a fcholarfhip, not exceeding five
years: what glorious effects then are to be
expected from his activity and zeal for the
fervice of his patron, in the future elections
of fuch fcholars, as will have votes at the
next general election for members of parliament! Of the feventy fcholars, thirty are
by the ftatutes allowed a more ample fubfiftence than the reft: and it is provided that
they fhall be all native Irifhmen. Thefe
thirty are called natives, and enjoy a yearly
falary, over and above their commons, of
twenty pounds. The vacancies amongft
them are filled up annually. The only qualifications which, heretofore, entitled a fcholar

to

to fucceed to a native's place, exclufive of
his being a native Irifhman, were feniority
and diligent attendance on College duties;
the fuperiority in learning of one fcholar
above another was never confidered; for all
fcholars, after their election, were looked upon, in refpect to their claims to College preferments, as equally learned : even in their
rank as fcholars they took place according to
their feniority, not according to the different degrees of learning they had manifefted,
on the examination preceding their election :
literary knowledge, fufficient to entitle a
man to a fcholarfhip, was looked upon as
fufficient to entitle him to any College emolument, ufually enjoyed by a fcholar: but
this equal method of diftribution of College
emoluments, which obviated the machinati-
on of partiality, was no way favourable to
electioneering operations. Mr. Hutchinfon,
on the diftribution of natives places, which
happened previous to the election of members of parliament, came to the board with
a long lift of new qualifications for a native's
place, read them to us, declared he was determined that no Scholar fhould be appointed to a native's place, who did not poffefs
all thefe qualifications, or at leaft a great
number of them : and then began to diftin-
guifh

guiſh the Scholars into various claſſes, as beſt
ſuited with his own views. If he had been
ſuffered to proceed, no Scholar, but ſuch as
had promiſed to vote for his Son, could
have obtained any of theſe places; for every
ſcholar in the oppoſite intereſt was excluded
by his want of one or other of theſe qualifications, which in general were abſurd and
ridiculous : but he had reaſons ready to offer, and very prolix ones, to excuſe the
want of them in all the others. The majority of the board, however, diſdained to be
cajoled by ſuch chicanery : he could not procure any Scholar to be elected, or rejected,
but on the footing of having, or wanting, the
two ancient accuſtomed qualifications of ſe-
niority and diligence, except one gentleman
(and in his caſe too he was driven to exerciſe his negative power) altho' he practiſed
more tricks, than a juggler at a country wake,
to avoid coming to that extremity : without
it, however, he could not effect his purpoſe;
for he had no power of nomination in this
caſe: he could prevent the board from electing, but could not fill up the vacancy without it's concurrence. This gentleman was
the Rev. Daniel Keller : a perſon of unblemiſhed reputation, a native Iriſhman, the
ſenior of the candidates for natives places,

and

and the moft diligent of them all in his attendance on College duties. As military
men, who have nothing to depend on but
their fwords, are called foldiers of fortune;
fo Mr. Keller may be ftyled a fcholar of fortune, having nothing whatfoever to depend
on for fubfiftence, but his learning. The
Provoft was particularly enraged againft
him, becaufe his known poverty rendering
him, in his opinion, vincible by promifes
of Collegiate emoluments, he had looked upon him as a certain voter for his fon; but
his poverty was a virtuous one, like that of
Cincinnatus; he difdained a bribe perhaps more
than thofe who poffefs thoufands; openly declared his intention to vote according to the
dictates of his honour and confcience, and de-
rided the attacks of the Provoft's agent. There
were, to the beft of my recollection, eight
natives places to be difpofed of, and the Provoft, tho' repeatedly called upon by feveral
members of the board, to put Mr. Keller in
nomination, at the difpofal of each of them,
arbitrarily, and in direct violation of his
duty, refufed to do fo: thereby preventing
the members from giving their votes, freely
and honeftly; and when the eighth and laft
was to be difpofed of, he put two or three
gentlemen fucceffively in nomination, who
were

were rejected by five of the board, the majority at the fame time declaring, that they
would not elect any one into the place, 'till
Mr. Keller was put in nomination : on which
the Provoft, finding them immovable, at
length declared, that he put his negative on
Mr. Keller: and then the board proceeded
to the election of another, quite contrary to,
my judgment, for I preferred the method of
letting the place lie vacant. Thus Mr. Keller
was deprived of a native's place, tho' entitled to it by the ftatutes, and the votes of the
board. The reader may judge how far the
Provoft's conduct to this poor gentleman was
confiftent with that prefcribed by the claufe
of his oath, which obliges him " To preferve
" the ftatutes of the College to the utmoft of
" his power, and to give his affent to all
" things which fhall be done according to their
" prefcriptions." His refentment had before
this induced him to behave in a moft arbitrary, unftatutable, and oppreffive manner
to Mr. Keller, who had never given him any
offence, except by refufing to vote for his fon.
A place of roll-keeper in the chapel became
vacant, worth 10l. a year; Mr. Daniel Keller
was elected into the place unanimoufly by the
board; there happened to be at that time in
the College one Jeremiah Keller, who was a
fcholar

scholar of the house ; the Rev. Doctor Forfayeth was then junior Dean, and had the
superintendance of these roll-keepers ; he
gave the roll to this Jeremiah Keller, and in-
sisted that the Provost designed it for Jeremiah, altho' Daniel Keller had been elected.
Daniel Keller came to me and informed me
of Doctor Forsayeth's behaviour, and I went
to the Provost to complain of it : he, to my
great surprise, told me, that he had designed the place for Jeremiah, that it was a
place in his gift, and that the appointment
of Daniel by the board was not valid, altho'
he had himself submitted it to the disposal
of the board, and tho' it was statutably
in the gift of the board, and not in
the Provost's. Jeremiah retained the
place, and voted for the Provost's son.
This cruel behaviour of the Provost, to Mr.
Keller, ought to have induced him rather
to favour, than oppress him further ; for
tho' he refused to vote for his son, yet his
spoils had bought a vote for him ; but the
aggressor never forgives: besides he could not
afford to waste any College emoluments on
the refractory ; they were all too little to sa-
tisfy the keen appetites of his friends. He
considered Mr. Keller also as a poor obscure
person, and that therefore it was not probable

ble his oppreffion of him could be attended with any confequences materially hurtful to his intereft. In refpect to premiums, where-ever he could interfere, he took care to make them fubfervient to his defigns : he had writ-ten and publifhed a moft ridiculous pamph-let, entitled, " Some regulations made in Trinity College, Dublin, fince the appoint-ment of the prefent Provoft." It fhould have been entitled, " Some projects defign-ed for execution in Trinity College, Dublin." The ftyle (if it deferves the name of ftyle) was inferior to that of * Twiss, and fcarce any of the projects it contained have yet been executed : but, like all mountebanks, he could not carry on trade without advertifing. In this pamphlet he afferts, that compofi-tion had not been fufficiently cultivated in the College, and then inferts an abfurd ad-vertifement, which he had caufed to be publifhed in the newfpapers, containing the methods which were hereafter to be purfued in the College, for the encouragement of compofition and elocution. He intended, by this part of his pamphlet, to make the pub-lick believe, that there was heretofore no en-couragement in the College for either; it being his conftant practice, wherever the

direct

* An illiterate buffoon, who has publifhed fome books of travels, particularly a book entitled a Tour thro' Ireland.

direct affertion of a falfehood would be en-
countered by as direct a negation, rather to
infinuate than affert it; and when the falfehood is expofed, if it be very fhameful and
notorious, he brings himfelf off with a declaration that he never afferted it. Compofition and elocution, before his elevation to
the Provoftfhip, were encouraged more than
they have been fince. Premiums were propofed for the beft compofitions, and conferred on the authors according to their merit;
and fuch gentlemen as pronounced publick
orations, were diftinguifhed with academick honours. Since his appointment, elocution has received no particular encouragement; the premiums, which have been diftributed to the authors of compofitions,
were difpofed of to promote his electioneering intereft, and gratify his vanity; and he
has taken care, that they fhall be difpofed of
for the future in fuch a manner as to ferve
thefe ends only. There has been but one
diftribution of thefe premiums, fince his appointment: the candidates were few; four
only obtained premiums, as well as I can recollect: two of them were trifling ones; the
two moft confiderable were given, one to his
fon, the candidate for reprefenting the College in parliament, and the other to a Scholar
of

of the Houſe, ſtaunch to his intereſt. As the
circumſtances attending this diſtribution
were very curious, I ſhall ſtate them particularly. The long vacation, when ſeveral
of the Senior Fellows were in the country,
was the time he fixed upon for the performance of this job, that Dr. Forſayeth before
mentioned, one of the Junior Fellows, and
his zealous partiſan, might be a member of
the board. Heretofore, the authors of compoſitions, who aſpired to premiums, were
obliged to ſend copies to all the members of
the board, with fictitious ſignatures, a fortnight at leaſt before the day fixed for the diſtribution, that each of the judges might
have ſufficient time to examine into the
merits of the performances, and to prevent
their being warped by any partiality to the
authors, who were not to be known till after the premiums were adjudged. On this
occaſion, no copies were ſent, except to the
Provoſt, and his confidant, Dr. Leland,
profeſſor of oratory ; neither was any day
fixed for the diſtribution; that depended on
the Provoſt's pleaſure and convenience.
When the board was aſſembled, which con-
ſiſted of the Provoſt, four Senior Fellows
and three Juniors, I was ſurpriſed to find a
parcel of compoſitions on the table, on whoſe
reſpective

respective merits the Provost declared w
were then to determine : it was impossibl
to read them, much less to judge of thei:
merits, on such short notice ; they were a
formidable heap. After several praises be-
stowed by Dr. Leland, on a bulky Latir
poem, said to contain the history of Joseph
the board was adjourned, I think, to the
next day, or the day after : the same Doctor
declaring, that he would send the compositions to be perused by the several members
of the board, in the mean time. It was impossible for the six members of the board, to
read and examine all the compositions with
attention and care, in less than twelve days,
allowing two days for each, as there was but
the one copy of each composition ; and they
must have been very diligent, if they could
have completed the business properly in
that time : whether they were, or were not
sent to the other members, I cannot tell,
but to me they were never sent ; and when
we next met to adjudge the premiums, I declared that I would not give any judgment,
as I never had read the compositions : the
Provost told me, that I might then read
them ; but I remarked that there was then
neither time nor opportunity for so doing,

and

and the firſt premium was immediately afterwards adjudged to the author of the Latin
poem before-mentioned. Dr. Leland declared
that the name of the author had been ſent to
him, encloſed in a billet ſealed up, and that
he did not know who he was; but, on open-
ing the billet, he proclaimed, with a burſt of
ſurprife and joy, that the author was the
Provoſt's ſon ; paid him the higheſt compliments on the amazing genius of his boy, and
acted the part aſſigned him in ſuch a ludicrous manner, as to make it evident to all
preſent, that he well knew the author of the
poem before the adjudication; which circumſtance was afterwards fully proved : and
it is highly probable, that there were other
members in the ſecret as well as Dr. Leland
but they were not ſo forward to expoſe
themſelves. This performance never afterwards ſaw the light: it was immediately
ſuppreſſed; and the Provoſt told us, with
great ſeeming concern, that it was loſt.
The conduct of him and his aſſociates, with
reſpect to the compoſition which obtained the
ſecond premium, was ſtill more barefaced:
this performance was an Engliſh poem, containing the ſtory of Orellana, taken from An-
ſon's voyage : copies of it had been ſent to
all the members of the board two years before,

fore, in the time of the late Provoſt ; and it had been then rejected by the board, as unworthy of any encouragement. I was a member of the board which rejected it, and was one of the majority ; but no member had declared his contempt of it ſo ſtrongly as Dr. Leland. His opinion was now much changed; he declared it had great merit, and that it was rejected ſolely by the authority of the late Provoſt, who would not ſuffer the board to give their judgment concerning it, though they had all thought that the author deſerved encouragement. His behaviour did not ſurpriſe me; I knew his character too well : but I did not think fit to ſuffer it to paſs unnoticed : I declared that the compoſition had been rejected by a majority, (for tho' no votes had been formally demanded, yet the majority had expreſſed their opinions) and that Dr. Leland himſelf had been one of that majority : that the compoſition in itſelf was contemptible, and beneath criticiſm : that, after a compoſition had been rejected by the board, it was very improper to obtrude it on the board again, particularly when two of the members, who had aſſiſted at the board, when it had been rejected, were abſent : and that the further conſideration of

its

its merit or demerit ought at leaft to be poftponed, until the two abfent gentlemen fhould
return to the College. But my objections
were fcarcely noticed ; the job had been already planned and fettled ; the fecond premium was adjudged to the author of it, whom
Dr. Forfayeth then declared to be his own
ward, and chamber-fellow, and who was a
fcholar of the houfe, zealoufly attached to
the Provoft's interefts : by fuch infamous
jobs as thefe has compofition been encouraged in the College fince Mr. Hutchinfon's
appointment. The two bulwarks, if I may fo
fay, of impartial judgment, to wit, the fur-
nifhing of the members of the board with copies, a reafonable time previous to the decifion on the refpective merits of the performances, and concealment of the authors until after the decifion, are both demolifhed ; and the
Provoft's laft advertifement, refpecting premiums for compofition, fhews that he intends
they fhould remain in ruins : for it has prefcribed, that copies of the performances fhall
be fent only to himfelf and Dr. Leland : thus
they will become rewards, not of genius, but
of electioneering fervice ; and the fum of 200l.
annually allotted, by the governors of Erafmus Smith's fchools, to be laid out in premiums for the encouragement of compofition,

L   in

in the College, will ferve only for the purpofes of corruption. It is to be hoped that the governors of Smith's fchools, or the Houfe of Commons, if they decline it, will make fome inquiry into the expenditure of this fund; and that they will not permit any part of this noble charity to be hereafter applied to the purchafing of feats in parliament, for Mr. Hutchinfon's children, by the corruption of the fcholars of the College. Mr. Hutchinfon's dexterity in rendering every thing which had any relation to the College, in fome fhape or other, fubfervient to his defigns on the late election, is not more remarkable, than his provident fagacity in fecuring an intereft on any future election by fimilar methods : his conduct, in the admiffion of Sizars into the College, is a rare inftance of his forefight in this refpect. The 19th chapter of the ftatutes ordains, " That the number of Sizars in the College fhall never exceed thirty ; that of thefe the Provoft fhall nominate eight, and each of the Fellows one, fo as exactly to complete the number : it had heretofore been cuftomary for the Senior Lecturer, on the Tuefday after Trinity Sunday annually, to examine all young perfons who appeared as candidates for Sizarfhips; and to fill up the vacancies with the beft anfwerers.

fwerers. The Provoft and Fellows heretofore tacitly waved their right of nomination, preferring the method of admiffion by examination, becaufe it excluded ignorance: But Mr. Hutchinfon paid no regard to the character, honour, or benefit of the College in this particular. He obferved that a confiderable number of Sizars obtained fcholarfhips, their poverty fharpening their induftry, and that therefore an intereft with them would be very ufeful to him on any future election; that they were all perfons, who had nothing to depend on for their fubfiftence, during their courfe of academick education, but the provifion which their learning might entitle them to from the College; and he concluded that neceffity would plead powerfully in his favour with fuch perfons, as they knew that no College emolument could be conferred without his concurrence: he remarked alfo that fuch Sizars as neglected their ftudies, and even many of them who had obtained fcholarfhips, being of low birth and breeding, and generally full-grown men, before they became members of the College, were the only perfons fit to be enlifted as effectives, or who would enlift, in the gang of defperadoes, now openly countenanced in the College, to terrify, menace, and infult every gentleman whofe dig-

nity,

nity, ftation, or fpirit made him obnoxious
to the Provoft; obfcurity, poverty, and low
breeding being fome of the neceffary qualities of a complete ruffian; the two firft rendering wicked men defperate, the laft, brutal.
To fecure the intereft then of this body, he
determined not only to exercife the power given him by the ftatute refpecting their admiffion, but to ftretch it beyond its limits :
and on the admiffion of Sizars, previous to
the election of members of parliament, there
being then fix or feven vacancies, he fent a lift
of names to the Senior Lecturer, previous to
the examination, with a note defiring him to
admit the perfons, therein named, Sizars : the
number of candidates was upwards of thirty; the feven nominated by the Provoft left
the Hall; and the Rev. Doctor Stokes, then
Senior Lecturer, moft unaccountably examined the remaining candidates, although
all the vacant Sizarfhips had been filled up
by the Provoft's nomination; and the unhappy gentlemen, who had been thus mock-
ed by a fruitlefs examination, twenty-four
in number, were fhortly afterwards informed
that there was no vacancy. Thus feven par-
tizans of the Provoft were at once obtruded
upon the College, to be hereafter fcholars
of the houfe, as we may reafonably conclude,
from the manner in which he conducted a
former

former election of fcholars, without its being known, whether they were at all qualified for admiffion, and to the prejudice, perhaps the ruin, of fome young men, whofe
circumftances rendered them unable to fupport the expenfes of a Collegiate education.
By the ftatute he has the power of nominating eight Sizars only, out of the thirty, fo
that by this exertion of his authority, in nominating feven at one time, he affumed a
greater power than was ftatutably vefted in
him; for as he chofe to break through the
old laudable cuftom of admitting Sizars on
examination, he ought not to have nominated
perfons to fill up more than one-fourth of
the vacancies at once, that being nearly the
proportion, which eight bears to thirty. His
conduct in this particular gave great offence to
the publick: it could not be concealed; there
were too many fufferers by it; it was expofed,
with all its odious circumftances, in the daily prints: he became uneafy; not from fhame
or remorfe, but becaufe he dreaded the effects
of popular refentment, and ftrove to difguife it:
with that view he ordered Dr. Stokes, about
a fortnight after the examination, to fend for
and admit five of the beft anfwerers amongft
the difcarded twenty-four candidates; and,
as the circumftance of the admiffion of Sizars, without any examination, had been fe-
verely

verely animadverted on, he directed the Doctor also to examine the seven nominees, not for the purpose of inquiring whether they were qualified for admission or not, as they were already admitted, but to give him an opportunity of asserting, that they had been examined; and thus, according to his custom, by concealing the most material part of the transaction, and telling an insignificant truth, he gained some colour for declaring that his enemies had maliciously traduced him; the nominated Sizars had indeed been examined, this he took pains to publish, but not previous to their admission; nor were they admitted on account of their superior skill; these circumstances he took care to conceal: by such cobweb blinds did he endeavour to screen his tyranny, from the publick eye. The statute, as I before mentioned, had positively enjoined,* that the number of Sizars should not exceed thirty; lest, as the statute expresses it, they should be a burthen to the College; this attempt, to disguise his guilt, made the number amount to thirty-six, and loaded the College with six supernumeraries, who remained a burthen on its funds, and on their brethren, (their general provision being scanty) 'till the next year, when the Supernumeraries were adopted into the vacant places, so that two Sizarships only were vacant on the

* See the College statutes, chapter 19th.

the following examination, although there
were above twenty candidates, and thefe
were vacated, by an extraordinary exertion of the authority of the board. Thus
fcholarfhips, natives-places, premiums, and
fizarfhips, were all made fubfervient to his
grand defign, of returning two of his creatures to parliament as reprefentatives of the
Univerfity. The purfuit of his fecond object, to wit, his gaining the reputation of a
learned man, very often placed him in a moft
ridiculous point of view : his weaknefs in
this particular was almoft infantine : he had
always at his tongue's-end the names of the
two famous Greek authors, Demofthenes and
Thucydides, whofe works, as I have before
fufficiently fhewn, he had never read; or if
he had, his memory muft have been extremely defective. Thefe he lugged in, head and
fhoulders, on all occafions. Did he talk of his
improvements at Palmerftown, of tranfactions in parliament, or at the bar, of his friend
Blacquiere, or the Miftrefs of Blacquiere,
his own honoured patronefs, or of any fubject whatfoever ? Demofthenes and Thucydides began or ended each fentence : yet
he had neither the ingenuity nor induftry of
the learned critick, defcribed in Swift's Rhap-
fody on Poetry : * he never ventured to quote

any

* Sometimes a learn'd critick dupes us,
With fham quotations, peri upfous ;

Then

any paſſage out of theſe authors, tho' I obſerved he had an Engliſh tranſlation of Thucydides in his chamber, probably he had never taken the trouble of reading even that :
but tho' Demoſthenes and Thucydides were his
coral and bells; yet he ſometimes played with
more dangerous things, and flouriſhed them
to the infinite detriment of the College. To
diſplay his own profound knowledge, he
ſuggeſted to every creature, who enjoyed the
happineſs of an eaſy familiarity with him,
the *ambubaiarum Collegii*, buffoons, mimicks,
&c. &c. &c. that the under-graduate courſe
of education in the College, was very defective in reſpect to the cultivation † of the *Belles
Lettres*, and ſuch of the *ambubaiæ*, as had
been bred at a grammar ſchool, actuated by
                                                      the

> Then, left with Greek he over run ye,
> Procure the book for love or money
> Tranſlated from Boileau's tranſlation,
> And quote quotation on quotation.
>   Rhapſody on Poetry.

† He has lately cauſed an advertiſement to be inſerted in the
publick prints, ſigned by the Senior Lecturer, but of his own
penning ; as the barbarous ſtyle of it ſufficiently demonſtrates ;
for he is as ignorant of the grammatical part of his own, as of
any other language ; and is unable to write a ſingle line of
Engliſh : in this he ſets forth, that a critical claſſical examination, was for the future to be held annually in the College,
and premiums to be diſtributed to the beſt anſwerers. This
publication ſerved two purpoſes ; one, to deceive the uninform-
ed multitude into an opinion, that he was making improvements in the courſe of education in the College ; the other,
that the ſtudy of the claſſicks had been neglected there, before
his promotion. Both theſe opinions are injurious to the College,
and can be ſupported only by falſehood and miſrepreſentation.
The higheſt encouragements had been, ever ſince the founda-
                                                      tion

the fame vanity, fuggefted to him fome alteration or other, which he greedily adopted as his own, immediately propofed it at the board, and recommended it as a confiderable improvement. Some of the board, whom he had gained over to his intereft by the means I fhall hereafter mention, defirous to make their court, by indulging his innovating humour, applauded, in the moft fulfome manner, every alteration he propofed : Dr. Leland particularly was always, on fuch occafions, *à facie jactare manus, laudare parat.†* His projected improvements, however, were feldom abfolutely adopted by the board; but lay over for further confideration : the only thing, generally, effected by the Provoft, was to prevail fo far, that the Greek and Latin authors hitherto appointed to be read by each clafs, preparatory to their refpective quarterly examinations, were repudiated, and no others fubftituted in their places; or at leaft fuch as were liable to change by the Senior Lecturer, at every quarterly examination. And Dr. Leland, who had been *Senior Lecturer* for a confiderable time, never thought fit to afcertain the books which were to be read by the Students of each clafs, previous

to

tion of the College, held forth to the proficients in claffical erudition. Scholarfhips and natives places, the next emoluments to fellowfhips, were appropriated to their reward and encouragement, and diftributed on annual examinations.

† With voice fonorous, and extended hands,
  Ready to flatter.

to each examination, or declined doing fo, until examinations were fo near, that a fufficient time was not left for the Students to prepare themfelves by ftudying the books appointed to be read. Incertainty has been the mother of idlenefs, and the under-graduates, or the greater part of them, have read few of the clafficks for this year paft and upwards, to their irreparable lofs: fo much eafier it is to demolifh than build! ‡ The writer of the life of that learned and pious prelate Dr. Bedell, Bifhop of Kilmore, obferves, that when he was appointed Provoft of Trinity College, Dublin, before his election to the Bifhop's Bench, he fpent a whole year in obferving and ftudying the conftitution of the College, then in its infancy, before he attempted to make the leaft alteration, although he was one of the moft learned men of his age, had been educated in the Univerfity of Cambridge, where he had fpent great part of his life, and was elected Provoft, by the intereft of Archbifhop Ufher, for the very purpofe of new-modelling the courfe of education : fuch was the caution and modefty of that venerable Bifhop! Mr. Hutchinfon, no member of any College,

‡ Such was the ftate of the College, when I refigned my fellowfhip, in June 1776: whether this has been fince remedied or not, I cannot certainly tell ; but I am inclined to believe that things remain in the fame ftate.

lege, and abfolutely illiterate, procures the Provoftfhip, by the corruption of a Lord Lieutenant's Secretary, at a time when the College had arrived at maturity, when it was filled with men of learning and abilities, when its courfe of education was in fuch efteem, that it was thought worthy of imitation, by the governors of fome of the moft diftinguifh- ed feminaries; * and propofes more alterations in this courfe of education, in the firft half year after his appointment, than had been made in a whole century before ; then pub- lifhes pompous accounts of them, in fwarms of pamphlets and advertifements. What a contraft ! But fuch conduct is not furprifing. Empyricks and mountebanks are always more defperate and noify than fkilful phyficians.

Mr. Hutchinfon's management of the Col- lege-funds comes next to be confidered; for I fhall delineate the outlines of his whole conduct in the government of the College, before I paint his particular behaviour to in- dividuals. Whilft the bargain and fale, rela- tive to the Provoftfhip, was in agitation be- tween him and the fecretary ; the latter, like a true jockey, to raife the terms of purchafe,

plained loudly that he had been bitten: but, however, to make the beft of a bad bargain, he fet himfelf vigoroufly to inquire into the circumftances of the College-eftate. The revenues of the College were amply fufficient to fupport the foundation; there was befides a confiderable annual faving; and the board heretofore, from time to time, raifed the rents in fuch a manner, that the increafe of their yearly income bore a juft proportion to the decreafe of the value of money, or, what is the fame thing, to the increafe of value of all neceffary commodities. But the children of this world are wifer in their generation than the children of light. Mr. Hutchinfon could eafily fee that the more he increafed the rents of the College, the greater would be his own income. The renewal fines always rife in proportion with the rent, and are divided into nine parts; two of thefe parts go into the Provoft's pocket, and one into that of each Senior Fellow; befides he confidered, if he could raife the annual income greatly beyond the expenfes of the College, he might, by force of mifreprefentation, and by the favour of the crown, the founder and patron of the College, obtain a large part of this redundancy to himfelf, as an additional falary; or, perhaps, procure an alienation of part of it, to fome of his children: and therefore, tho' the increafe of rents was, at the time of his

appointment,

appointment, the common calamity of the
tenantry of this nation, and had caufed dangerous infurrections (particularly in the northern parts, where the College had large eftates) which were followed by migrations of
thoufands of the peafants and manufacturers
to America, yet, in this very feafon of difcontent and diftrefs, did he refolve to increafe the
rents of the College-lands.   There had been
a general furvey and valuation of thefe eftates
in the year 1717. The value of lands had certainly rifen greatly fince that period : but
the board had, in all their late demifes, confidered the value of all their eftates, as much
greater than that valuation rated them, and
increafed their rents accordingly. This did
not content him : he caufed a new-furvey and
valuation to be made, which coft the College near two thoufand pounds : this furvey
was entirely ufelefs, the former being extremely accurate ; and it was projected by
him, with the defign of racking the tenantry
for his own emolument. It had indeed been
alleged, by way of apology for his putting
the College to this enormous expenfe, and
in defence of the new valuation, that feveral
large tracts of land, which, at the time of
the former furvey, were entirely wafte and
uncultivated, were now rendered profitable
by the induftry of the under-tenants; that
the

the immediate tenants of the College had not
been at any expenfe in reclaiming fuch
grounds, and that therefore they ought now
to pay rent for them, as well as for the
other parts of the College-lands, which they
refpectively held. This is a fpecious way of
reafoning, which has only the appearance
of ftrength : as the College, like other ecclefiaftical corporations, can grant no leafe
for a longer term than 21 years, the tenantry,
without fome encouragement, would neglect
the improvement of the land : hence, as well
from neceffity as principles of juftice, one
maxim was adopted, viz. in the valuation
of College-lands, never to value the tenant's
improvements : I believe it will be hardly
controverted, that the reclaiming of barren
land, and rendering it profitable, is an improvement ; therefore, this argument, in favour of a new furvey, has no weight. It ac-
quires no additional ftrength from the affertion, that the immediate tenant of the College has been at no expenfe in this improvement ; for the tenant and under-tenant are
to be confidered, by the landlord, as one and
the fame perfon. The under-tenant is, in refpect to the landlord, as it were, the fervant of
the immediate tenant ; for whom he is only
anfwerable to the landlord, and it cannot be
alleged that the landlord has been at the expenfe

penfe of making the improvement, and therefore he ought not, in juftice, to benefit further by it, than as an additional fecurity to him for the punctual payment of his rent. Ecclefiaftical corporations, and particularly the College, ought to confider the eftates they poffefs, not as the private property of the individuals which compofe them, but as revenues. with which they are endowed by the laws of the land, to enable them to carry into execution the purpofes, for which they were firft inftituted ; and confequently ought not to rack their tenantry, to pamper the luxury of their conftituent parts, when the rents, already payable, are more than fufficient to anfwer all the ends of their eftablifhment. But Mr. Hutchinfon was deaf to all arguments, againft raifing the College-rents, arifing either from juftice, reafon, or publick convenience ; and abfolutely refufed renewing any College-leafe, (no leafe being valid without his confent) but on the terms of a great increafe in the rent. The immediate tenant being thus loaded with an heavier rent than heretofore, and unwilling to fubmit to a decreafe of his profit, raifed the rents of his under-tenants, the actual land-holders, in proportion : and hence refulted beggary, difcontent, and migration, throughout the College-eftates, without any benefit whatfoever

foever to the fociety. To glofs over his conduct, in this particular, he alleges, that he
has many fchemes to execute for the improvement of the College, which will require a confiderable additional income : but
if thefe fchemes are the whims, of which he
has given an account to the Publick, in the
pamphlet I have already mentioned, or fimilar to them, they are not only, generally,
ufelefs, but fome ridiculous, fome mifchievous, and others impracticable. And if *Al-
ma Mater* ever happens to be tricked out in
fuch frippery attire, fhe will appear more
like the diffolute and abandoned harlot, than
the modeft, fober matron. It has been mentioned, and truly, that the buildings in the
College are not large enough to fupply lodgings for the body, and that fome part of
them are decayed, others too mean, particularly the chapel, and out of character with
the reft of the edifice. Large and expenfive ad-
ditions and repairs are certainly neceffary : the
parliament had, in the time of the late Provoft, and before, granted very great fums
for rebuilding the College, and no lefs a fum
than £12,000 of this money is ftill unexpended : this fum is fufficient to rebuild
the chapel, and fuch part of the front
court, as has been left unfinifhed. Buildings neceffary for the accommodation of
fuch

fuch of the body, as want of lodgings had excluded from refidence within the College, may be erected out of the prefent redundancy of the annual income, and other funds in the poffeffion of the College, and this redundancy, by the wife and juft provifions of the board before Mr. Hutchinfon's appointment, and without the aid of his exactions on the tenants, was every day increafing: fome time before the late Provoft's death, it was agreed upon by the Board, to erect an additional building, the eftimate of the expenfe of which did not amount to £4000, which would have conveniently lodged fifty Students and two Fellows. The erection of this building was prevented by Mr. Hutchinfon, becaufe its intended fituation precluded it from ever forming any part of a new regular Court. However it is evident from this eftimate, that the fum of £8000 would fupply the expenfe of erecting buildings fufficient to afford lodgings to all Students now excluded, who are defirous of refiding in the College: their number not exceeding one hundred; as many Students chufe to refide in town with their parents and friends. The fum already faved out of

M the

the College income, the accruing favings, and a very large fum of Money bequeathed to the College by Provoft Baldwin, compofe a fund more than doubly fufficient to fupport this expenfe: fo that the reafons advanced by Mr. Hutchinfon and his adherents, for the neceffity of raifing the College rents, in a much greater proportion than was heretofore ufual, particularly at fo calamitous a feafon, arc all weak and fallacious: the real motive of his conduct in this refpect, is, the emolument of himfelf and his family. After he had procured the confent of the Board to the execution of the new furvey and valuation, which coft the College, as I before mentioned, about £2000, he informed them, that the Provoft's houfe was too fmall for his accommodation, and requefted that they wou'd agree to defray the expenfe of an enlargement of it, which he afferted would not coft more than £300, but which I believe will be hardly completed for double the fum, and readily obtained their confent: this was an unneceffary expenfe, for the Provoft's houfe was almoft new, fpacious and magnificent, and the erection of it coft no lefs than £11,000, fhortly before

his

his appointment. His next job was the procuring an ample yearly penfion, out of the College funds, for one of his dependants. This man is named Myers; he had been a joiner at Whitehaven in England, but finding it convenient to repair to Ireland, he has for fome years refided here: Mr. Hutchinfon had obtained for him a lucrative place under government, as an architect, and he was now determined that he fhould fhare with him in the fpoils of the College. He celebrated this cabinet-maker's fkill in architecture to the Board as no way inferior to that of Vitruvius, Palladio, or Jones, and defired that they would agree to his being appointed architect to the College, with an annual falary : it was objected, that there were no buildings then erecting in the College, and that it would be time enough to appoint a falary for an architect, or rather an overfeer, when the work was actually commenced. This was a reafonable objection, as it has been agreed at the Board to employ Sir William Chambers, to draw a plan of the intended buildings, but it was quickly overruled, and as it was afferted by the Provoft, that 5 per cent. on the mo-

ney

ney expended in building was ufually allowed to the architect, his propofal that
Myers fhould be paid an annual falary of
£150 by the College, in lieu of fuch allowance, was agreed to; and this man has enjoyed the falary now for two years and upwards, although no building whatfoever has
been carried on in the College during that
time, except the addition to the Provoft's
houfe, which by eftimate is to coft but £300.
It is neceffary to remark, that the moft opu-
lent and refpectable architect in Dublin in his
time, the late —— Darley efq. received but
£60 per annum from the College for fuper-
intending the College buildings and £20
per annum for reviewing the workmens accounts, at a time when the front court was
rebuilding, and when forty thoufand Pounds,
the bounty of parliament, were expended on
it; which falaries were ftopped immediately,
when the progrefs of the work was interrupted: and alfo, that Myers's annual falary
is nearly four times as much as the falary of a
junior Fellow, and much greater than that
of a fenior Fellow. But this man is ufeful
to the Provoft; he retains him as a witnefs,
and conftantly fends for him, when he is
about

about performing any action, for which he is likely to be cenfured, or called to account, that he may have the benefit of his friend-ly teftimony on the occafion. As Mr. Hutchinfon obferved, with a very curious eye, even the moft minute things belonging to the College, which he might convert to his advantage; he did not overlook the College plate; of this there was a very con-fiderable quantity, confifting chiefly of large pieces, the donations of feveral benefactors, whofe names and arms were engraved on the pieces refpectively: He immediately for-med the fcheme of converting this plate into an elegant table fervice for himfelf, and employed his trufty friend Doctor Leland to propofe at the Board, that the plate fhould be all melted down, and worked into a modern table-fervice; with which motion (as it was ftrongly fupported by the Provoft) the Board complied. The new fafhioning of it put the College to the expenfe of near four hundred pounds, and when the work was finifhed, the plate was carried to the Provoft's country-houfe at Palmerftown, where it has been fince conftantly ufed at his table. How conformable this conduct is

M 3   to

to the injunctions of the statutes, any one may judge from the following translation of a clause in the 19th chapter " let gold and " silver vessels and every thing else which " is precious, and is not in daily use, be " preserved in the common chest, and let " them be never taken out of it unless the " articles which are taken out be written " down in another register, to be kept by " the Provost, by the hand of the person " who takes them out, and unless a proper " security for the indemnity of the College * " be given." Doctor Andrews, the late Provost, sometimes used part of this plate at his table, but it was in the College, from which he never removed it, nor did he ever alter its fashion, efface the memorials of the donors, and obliterate the marks by which it might be known to be College property. What security the College has for the faithful return of this plate, in case of Mr. Hutchinson's death, I know not; but it is pretty certain that it is very scanty and precarious, if there is any at all. I shall conclude

---

* See the Provost's oath. " I will preserve and administer all the benefices &c. and all the goods in general of said College, without diminution or waste."

conclude this account of his management of the property of the College with a hint to the reader, to compare the feveral facts I have ftated relative to his adminiftration of that property, with a part of the Provoft's oath which prefcribes a rule for his conduct in that particular. Mr. Hutchinfon obferved too, with even a microfcopick exactnefs, every minute thing belonging to the College, which could in any fhape, or by any means, be turned to the emolument of his dependants. The place of cook to the College, fome time after his appointment, became vacant. He had in his fervice a Swifs or a Frenchman called Auguftin Gaure, or Gare; this fellow, as I have been well informed, was brought up to the trade of a hair-dreffer; but he ferved the Provoft in the double capacity of houfe-fteward and butler, and his wife was a fort of an upper fervant and confidante to Mrs. Hutchinfon: the Provoft had taken care to procure him a poft in the revenue, probably in lieu of wages, and, immediately after his own appointment to the Provoftfhip, promoted him to the place of beadle of the Univerfity, worth about £20 per annum. The duty of

his

his employment in the revenue required his whole time and attention, if executed properly; for he is an officer, whose station is at Palmerstown, about three miles from Dublin, to prevent smuggling by land-carriage. On the death of the late College-cook, the Provost immediately recommended Gare to the Board, as a proper person to succeed him; and he was appointed, tho' some men regularly educated to the trade of cookery, and well recommended, had offered themselves candidates for the place: and now the list of Mr. Gare's promotions is almost as bulky as that of his patron. This hair-dresser is house-steward and butler to the Provost, (for these employments he still exercises with as much attention as ever) cook to the College, beadle to the University, and a land-carriage officer in his Majesty's revenue, whose station is at least five miles from the College. It has been alleged in parliament by the servants of the Crown, as a reason for demanding additional supplies, and creating new taxes, that the revenue of this kingdom has of late years fallen short of its usual amount: if the fact be true, it may very easily be accounted for, by supposing

that

that the commiffioners of the revenue appoint officers, to prevent frauds in the collection of it, equally unable to attend their duty with Mr. Gare: the execution of his duty of cook alone (if duly performed) without taking into confideration the duties of his employments of houfe-fteward, butler, and beadle, being fufficient to confume his whole time and attention, and he is pretty well paid for his trouble by the emoluments of the place, which amount to £200 per annum.

To perfons unacquainted with the conftitution of this College it may appear furprifing, that Mr. Hutchinfon has been able to prevail on the majority of the Board to concur in fo many things, evidently injurious and difgraceful to the Society: but it muft be confidered, that a moft enormous power, both in rewarding and punifhing, is given to the Provoft by the ftatutes, and that this power, formidable in itfelf, muft acquire tenfold ftrength, if placed in the hands of a man void of confcience, honour, or underftanding. Good fenfe may fometimes reftrain a wicked tyrant from outrageous exertions of

his

his power; and hence has arisen the obser-
vation, the truth of which experience has
proved, that the greatest mischiefs have been
executed by Fools; as weapons in the hands
of a mad man are more dangerous, than
when they are wielded by men in their reason.
This consideration alone may account for the
complaisance of the Board to Mr. Hutchinson;
but he made use of other engines also, to se-
cure the concurrence of a majority of its
Members with his measures: some of them
had been privately married, before he was
appointed Provost, and there is a clause in
the 7th chapter of the statutes, of which the
following is an exact translation: " If it be
" found out, that any of the Fellows or
" Scholars has taken a wife, or contracted
" matrimony with any woman, it is our
" pleasure that he be deprived of all Right
" of the Society." This clause kept them in
continual apprehension of a discovery of their
marriages, and caused them to entertain, with
the highest delight, any hopes whatsoever of
a mitigation of the severity of the statute in
this particular. These hopes and fears Mr.
Hutchinson turned to his own advantage.
His emissaries, and even his wife and family,

denounced

denounced vengeance publickly againſt all married Members of the College who ſhould préſume to oppoſe him : and he himſelf applied to the Lord Lieutenant, and procured a diſpenſation (by virtue of the Crown's diſpenſing power reſerved in the College charter) to ſhield Doctors Leland and Dabzack, two of his moſt active ſervants, whoſe ſervices even outſtripped and prevented his deſires, from the penalty annexed to marriage by the ſtatutes, with the avowed deſign of attacking the other married Members of the College, when he had ſecured his own minions from danger. This deſign his creatures have ſince thought fit to deny, with what degree of truth the reader may judge from the following circumſtances. William Clement, Eſq; M. D. the preſent Vice-provoſt of the College, has been in that ſtation for four-and-twenty years paſt; it being uſual annually to elect the Senior of the Senior Fellows into that place. This gentleman was a married man at the time of Mr. Hutchinſon's promotion, and, being a perſon of moſt unblemiſhed character, had been elected, in two ſucceſſive parliaments, one of the repreſentatives of the city of

Dublin

Dublin : when the Provoſt applied to Earl Harcourt for diſpenſations in reſpect to marriage for Doctors Leland and Dabzack, his Excellency told him, that he would procure them, but that he muſt alſo procure one for Doctor Clement at the ſame time ; he was induced to extend the privilege to Doctor Clement, not from any motives of regard, but merely from the apprehenſion of popular reſentment, if he was paſſed over on ſuch an occaſion ; for his matrimonial connexion was very publickly known, and his integrity had endeared him to the citizens of Dublin, who would not fail to reſent any indignity thrown on their favourite. The Provoſt oppoſed this reſolution in favour of Doctor Clement with all his might ; nothing could be more prejudicial to his views than ſuch a ſtep : the Doctor being the oldeſt Member of the Board, and a man of dignity and weight, was a ſort of check to his career of deſtruction, and he had formed the plan of awing him with the terrors of the ſtatute reſpecting marriage : he had even carried his petulance and audacity ſo far, as once to reprove this venerable old gentleman for being abſent from chapel. The

reſolution

refolution * of the Viceroy, therefore, in his favour, filled him with rage; he remonftrated as violently as he dared, but the Viceroy's determination was not to be changed ; he told him that he would procure difpenfations for the three or for none : and Mr. Hutchinfon was at length obliged to acquiefce. The fecurity of his two favourites was abfolutely neceffary, and there were other Fellows, tho' Doctor Clement fhould be placed out of his reach, who would be left expofed to the exertions of his vengeance on the fcore of marriage. Exclufive of the malignity of his intention in procuring thefe difpenfations, in what light muft his conduct appear, when compared with that claufe of the Provoft's oath which refpects difpenfations ? Such a comparifon will demonftrate, that no confiderations are fufficient to curb him in the purfuit of his revenge or intereft. Another circumftance, which will explain his intention

in

* The tranfactions between Lord Harcourt and Mr. Hutchinfon, on this occafion, have been told me by the higheft authority in this kingdom, excepting the prefent Lord Lieutenant; but the reader will obferve, that they do not admit of pofitive proof, as the other facts, I have fet forth, do ; being tranfactions which Lord Harcourt and Blacquiere only can prove directly.

in procuring thefe difpenfations, as much as
his oppofition to Doctor Clement's being
made an object of his Majefty's favour, is
the following : immediately after they were
granted, and before any account of them had
tranfpired, a gentleman, high in office under
the Crown, and in the greateft confidence
with government, defired me to be particularly careful in the point of marriage, as
fome defigns of a dangerous nature were
projected againft me, Mr. Hutchinfon and I
being then on very ill terms, and this gentleman, from rumour, fufpecting that I was
obnoxious to his power on that account:
And the Attorney general, under the fame
perfuafion, fhortly afterwards fent for me,
and told me that he would exert his intereft
to obtain a fimilar difpenfation for me : I
declined his kind offices in my own behalf,
but took the opportunity of recommending
to his protection three of the Junior Fellows,
whom I knew to ftand in need of fuch a
favour, and whom I then thought to be the
only Members of the College in that predi-
cament: with one of thefe gentlemen he was
not acquainted, and very flightly with the
others ; but his own benevolence, and their
danger,

danger, were fufficient incentives to induce him to exert his influence; he folicited and obtained fimilar difpenfations for them, maugre all the oppofition given by the Provoft and his Patrons to this meafure in England: And thus thefe gentlemen were faved from ruin, to the infinite mortification of him and his partifans, who, though they could not at the time conceal their grief and difappointment, yet have the impudence now to deny the defign of ruining the married Fellows, when the execution of fuch a fcheme is no longer in their power: thus the garb of innocence is affumed by the malicious, becaufe they are impotent. Whether difpenfations, in refpect of marriage, be hurtful or not to the intereft of the College, has been a point much agitated; but without confidering the Provoft's defigns, and the breach of his duty in procuring them, I can point out one great mifchief to the College, which is a confequence of this meafure; the Senior Fellows, defirous of marrying, were heretofore very ready to accept of fuch benefices, in the patronage of the College, as became vacant, and on fuch preferments to refign their Fellowfhips,

by

by which means the Junior Fellows succeeded into their places according to their rank. These dispensations to the doctors Leland and Dabzack will prevent their ever quitting the College, few livings in the gift of the Society being equally valuable with a senior Fellowship; and if the Provost should procure similar dispensations for all persons, who shall in time succeed to senior Fellowships, and shew themselves as alert in his service, as these two gentlemen, the Board will shortly be composed of his creatures only, who will hold their places for their lives. The use he will make of such a Board, the reader, from what I have already set forth, may easily conjecture; it is true, benefices in the gift of the College will be frequently conferred on junior Fellows; but the kingdom will be materially injured, by the ruin of its only Seminary of learning, which will be thus delivered up to a garbled junto, whose leader, by allowing a small portion of the emoluments to his crew, will be enabled to convert almost its whole property to his own purposes. The Board from such motives, and by such means as I have mentioned, being rendered obedient to his dictates

tates in moſt things, he ſeized the opportunity, during the firſt Chriſtmas vacation
after his appointment, when the reverend
Doctor Kearney and I were in the country,
and Doctor Forſayeth (for whom he had procured a church living from government,
concerning which I ſhall have occaſion to
ſpeak hereafter) was a member of the Board,
on account of our abſence, to draw up, and
read to the Board, a moſt fulſome eulogium
of himſelf, which he requeſted that the
Board would approve of, and inſert in the
College regiſtry as their act: A great majority of them being then his creatures, the
few, who diſapproved of ſuch a meaſure, were
ſilent; the panegyrick was inſerted, and is a
rare monument as well of his cunning, as
his impudence.

Having thus faithfully ſtated Mr. Hutchinſon's conduct in the government of the
College, and the adminiſtration of its revenues, and property; I ſhall lay before the
publick a few inſtances of the behaviour of
him and his partiſans to particular members
of the ſociety, which will ſerve further to
illuſtrate the man's temper and deſigns, and

N   explain

explain and prove feveral of my affertions in refpect to the motives of his conduct. I fhall begin with an account of his behaviour to —— Prefton, mafter of arts. This gentleman was one of the unfuccefsful candidates for a Fellowfhip, at the election which happened immediately previous to the promotion of Mr. Hutchinfon: on the examination which preceded that election, Mr. Prefton and four others appeared as candidates, though there was but one vacancy. All the five difplayed fuch learning on this examination, that the whole audience regretted the impoffibility of rewarding them all, fuitably with their merit: one only could fucceed. Mr. Prefton determined on the next election again to aim at the attainment of that preferment, to which his learning and induftry gave him fo reafonable a claim: Above four months before the time appointed by the ftatutes, for the filling-up vacant Fellowfhips, a church living in the patronage of the College became vacant. On the vacancy of fuch a living, it is the eftablifhed cuftom, for the Board to prefent fome one of the Fellows, making the firft offer to the fenior, who, when he is infti-

tuted

tuted and inducted, refigns his Fellowſhip.
The reverend Doctor Stokes had agreed to
accept this living; but as it is uſual to permit the Fellow, who accepts of a vacant
living, to remain five months in the College
after the vacancy, before it is expected that
he ſhould apply for inſtitution and induction,
doctor Stokes's Fellowſhip, if this general
uſage was to be exactly preſerved and infiſted
on, would not become vacant until ſome
ſhort time after the day of annual election;
the merits however of the unſuccefsful candidates on the former election, every one of
whom had determined to ſuſtain another
examination on any future vacancy, in hopes
of better fortune, had been ſo great and con-
ſpicuous, that the Board (Doctor Dabzack
being a member thereof) determined to preſent Doctor Stokes to the benefice, ſo long
before the time of the annual election of
Fellows, as that he might procure inſtitution
and induction, and reſign his Fellowſhip,
before that time. The untimely death of
the reverend Mr. Shewbridge, one of the
junior Fellows, after this determination,
made an unexpected vacancy. One of the
unſuccefsful candidates, on the former exami-

nation,

nation, had fo far outftripped his competi-
tors, that it was morally certain he would be
the beft anfwerer on the approaching one;
it was alfo as certain that Mr. Prefton would
be the next in merit, fo that if there fhould
be a fecond vacancy he would be elected a
Fellow: Unfortunately for Mr. Prefton he
had the reputation of being a poet, and fame
reported him to be the author of fome ingenious fatirical pieces ridiculing the Provoft's abfurdities; he affociated alfo with
men, who did not favour his electioneering
views: thefe were circumftances fufficient to
make the Provoft his implacable enemy, and
though he had no foundation for his refentment againft him except common report, he
determined that Mr. Prefton fhould not be
elected a Fellow: But as he was by this time
become extremely unpopular, he was afraid
of increafing the publick indignation, by the
open exertion of his negative power againft
Mr. Prefton: He determined therefore that
Doctor Stokes fhould not refign his Fellowfhip until after the election; although it had
been before determined that he fhould refign
before, as I have already mentioned. Exclufive of his influence over Doctor Stokes, who
was

was a married man, and of a timid difpofition, and who, if he had not been in fuch
circumftances, yet might be juftly afraid to
difoblige him on this occafion, as his prefen-
tation could not be valid without his confent,
he had a ready inftrument in doctor Dabzack
to affift in the execution of the fcheme.
This gentleman, on Stokes's refignation,
was to fucceed to the place of a fenior
Fellow, being fenior of the juniors; and the
Provoft had fo contrived matters, that Dabzack fhould infift on enjoying the full emoluments of a fenior Fellow, from the time of
Stokes's refignation, and that Stokes fhould
therefore infift on retaining his Fellowfhip,
until the laft hour which cuftom had limited
for his refignation; unlefs Dabzack, if he
refigned immediately, would confent to allow him thefe emoluments, as if he had
continued a Fellow, until the cuftomary
time of refignation. This fcheme was executed in all its parts with great formality;
both gentlemen remained obftinate in their
demands; doctor Stokes's Fellowfhip was not
refigned until about a fortnight after the
annual time of election; and Mr. Prefton,
who, as was eafily forefeen, was the fecond

in merit on the examination, was debarred
from a Fellowſhip, for the attainment of
which he had laboured inceſſantly during a
courſe of ſome years, and to which his great
erudition, unblemiſhed character, and innocence of life, moſt juſtly entitled him; and
a Fellowſhip remained vacant almoſt a whole
year to the injury of the College. Doctor
Stokes had ſome qualms of conſcience whilſt
this ſcheme was in execution; he made a
publick offer to ſubmit his claim to the arbi-
tration of the other ſenior Fellows, to abide
by their determination, and to reſign his
Fellowſhip, previous to the election; but
this offer was rejected by doctor Dabzack,
as it would have overturned the Provoſt's
project, although, if his claim had been
eſtabliſhed in its greateſt extent, the benefit
reſulting to him would not amount to forty
pounds, and as Doctor Stokes perſiſted in
his claim (with great reaſon and juſtice on
his ſide, if the matter in diſpute had been
conſiderable enough to warrant his retention
of his Fellowſhip, to the excluſion of a man
of exemplary merit from a proviſion for life)
Doctor Dabzack did not gain one farthing
but acted gratuitouſly in this ſhameful affair;
demon-

demonftrating to the world, that the Provoft
exacted the fame degree of obedience from
his creatures, which the prince of the af-
faffins in Paleftine did from his fubjects,
who ftabbed or precipitated themfelves or
others according to his orders. The Provoft
himfelf after expofing two of his adherents
to publick odium, for the parts they had acted, did not reap all the advantage he propofed
to himfelf from their difgrace; becaufe all
perfons acquainted with the College ftatutes
well knew, that it lay in his own power to
compel Doctor Stokes to refign his Fellowfhip at any time he thought proper, only by
declaring that if he did not immediately
refign, he would not agree to his prefenta-
tion. The daily enormities of Mr. Hutchinfon in the government of the College, his
flagrant violations of the ftatutes, and oppreffion of individuals, could not efcape the
obfervation of the publick; fcarce a day
paffed, but the prefs expofed fome inftance
of his tyranny and injuftice. Thefe publications tormented him; he conceived the
moft furious projects of revenge againft the
publifhers; and though he had began this
paper war himfelf, by an effay, ftuffed with

falfehoods,

falſehoods, and ſigned Moderator, as before
mentioned, printed in the Hibernian Journal,
one of the weekly news-papers, yet he
quickly found his weakneſs and inferiority
in a literary combat, and had ſufficient
cauſe to repent of his having commenced
hoſtilities. His rage and folly ſuggeſted
many ſchemes to him for ſilencing the
enemy's batteries, but none ſeemed ſo effectual, or ſuited ſo well with his temper and
underſtanding, as a perſonal attack on Mr.
Michael Mills, the printer of that deteſted
journal. In a dark evening in winter, a
choſen band of ruffians, armed with ſwords
and piſtols, ſallied forth from the College, to
the ſhop of Mr. Mills in Capel-Street, in the
city of Dublin; dragged him into a coach;
conveyed him to the College; knocked him
down under the pump, and would have
certainly murdered him, if ſome of the
Students, hearing the uproar, had not ran
out of their chambers, and reſcued him
from theſe aſſaſſins, who, finding their wicked
intentions fruſtrated, made their eſcapes;
they did not however retreat with ſuch
activity, but that ſome of them were obſerved and known. Mr. Mills complained

to

to the Board of this daring outrage; appeared and proved the fact againſt two Students; one of whom only the Provoſt would ſuffer to be academically puniſhed; the other was afterwards indicted, tried, and convicted for the fact, on the very ſame evidence which Mr. Mills had given at the Board, and puniſhed by the juſt ſentence of a court of law. The caſe of the Student, on whom the Provoſt thought it prudent to ſuffer an academick puniſhment to fall, deſerves par-ticular notice: he was an idle, thoughtleſs young fellow, of but middling underſtanding, and was rather weak than wicked; his idleneſs had incenſed his friends on whom he depended for his ſupport, having no ſub-ſiſtence whatſoever but from their bounty. He had, at the time he engaged in this enterprize, no means of reconciling his friends to him, or of procuring any future proviſion in life, except the obtaining of his degree of Batchelor of Arts, for which he was then a candidate: the hopes of ſucceſs were faint, his idleneſs having in a good meaſure diſabled him from ſuſtaining the examination, which always precedes the acquiſition of a Batchelor's degree. His

ſituation

fituation and purfuits were well underftood in the College, and one Anthony Gordon, a fcholar of the houfe, in great confidence with the Provoft, knowing him to be
a ftout able young man, and being defirous
of enlifting him, promifed, in the Provoft's
name, that if he would engage in the attack
on Mills, the degree fhould be conferred on
him. This the young man difcovered,
after the fact was committed, to his tutor,
the reverend Mr. Drought, one of the Fellows, and Mr. Drought immediately informed the Provoft of Gordon's promife, who
contented himfelf with fending Gordon,
a few hours after, to Mr. Drought, to deny
that he had ever made fuch a promife in
the Provoft's name: what degree of credit
is due to Gordon's teftimony, the publick
may judge. The young fellow afterwards
fuftained the examination for his degree,
but was rejected by the examiner; the Provoft at the Board, in fupport of Gordon's
promife, endeavoured to procure him his
degree notwithftanding; but, being informed that no fuch ftep had ever been taken in
the College, ordered his tutor to tell him,
that if there had been any example of a
perfon

perſon in his circumſtances having obtained
a degree, he ſhould have obtained one, and
that the Board did not refuſe him his degree, on account of the academick puniſhment he had ſuffered for aſſaulting Mills,
but for want of ſufficient learning. The
puniſhment itſelf was of an extraordinary
nature. The ſentence, inſerted in the College regiſtry, contained the moſt virulent
abuſe of Mr. Mills, the complainant, and
was drawn up by doctor Leland; it even
juſtified the aſſault, though at the cloſe it
contained the uſual form of admonition:
It is to be remarked alſo, that the Student
admoniſhed was not a ſcholar of the houſe,
and therefore had no vote on the election
of members of parliament, and that all his
friends, and connexions, were perſons, who
by no means favoured the Provoſt's deſigns.
And that the Student * acquitted by the
Board, or rather by the Provoſt, and afterwards found guilty by a jury, for the ſame
offence, on the ſame evidence, was a ſcholar
of

---

* This gentleman has been ſince rewarded for his ſervices
with a Fellowſhip; almoſt every one of his aſſociates are gratified with ſome Collegiate emolument or other. The rewards of
learning are turned into premiums for the dexterous management of the ſword, pump, and piſtol, in the Provoſt's quarrels.

of the houfe, a ftaunch voter for the Provoft's
fon, and all his friends were the Provoft's
creatures. It may not be amifs here to
ftate feveral outrages committed by this
gang, and the countenance and protection
the members of it received from the Provoft,
fince I have entered on the fubject ; although
other inftances of his conduct, which I fhall
mention, may have the priority in point of
time. On the day of election of members of
parliament, the Provoft himfelf being the
returning officer, two of the choiceft ruffians, who excelled all the reft in favage behaviour and brutality, were ftationed in
the hall, having received proper inftructions
for their conduct. After the poll had been
taken by the Provoft, and many of the voters
had left the hall, the Provoft read over the
lift of the voters, and each of thefe two
men made objections to the votes of feveral
of the Fellows and fcholars, though no objection had been made when they refpectively voted: under colour of thefe objections, they moft villanoufly traduced the cha-
racters of feveral of the Fellows, in the
oppofite intereft to that of the Provoft ;
boldly afferting the moft fcandalous falfehoods, without attempting the leaft proof of
them :

them : knowing themfelves, by his protection, fecure from any Collegiate punifhment;
and thinking themfelves fecure from actions
at law, as well by the provifions of the ftatutes, which forbid all fuits at law, between the members of the College, without
the confent of the Board; as by the privileges of voters on elections. Their flanders
and malignity feemed to be particularly
levelled at the reverend Mr. Torrens and
me. One of them had the infolence to
abufe the Attorney general in a grofs manner to his face, and continued this abufe
unreproved by the Provoft. The reverend
Mr. Ellifon, who was then junior Dean,
(and, from his office, the perfon whofe duty
it was to fuperintend the difcipline of the
College) though he had voted for the Provoft's fon, yet could not contain his indignation at the indecency of this conduct,
not of the ruffian, for he was only acting
the part affigned him, but of the Provoft,
who thus not only fuffered one of the moft
refpectable perfonages in the whole kingdom
to be infulted, but was really guilty of the
outrage himfelf, as it was offered by one
of his own party, in his prefence, and evidently with his approbation. He exclaimed
" that

" that the fellow deferved to be turned out
" of the hall ;". on which the Provoft, in a
furious manner, vociferated, " who will
turn him out ?" to which Mr. Ellifon anfwered " I will." This had the effect of
immediately ftopping the further effufion
of the fellow's venom : but Mr. Ellifon did
not efcape infult afterwards on this account.
The Provoft was obliged to repair to Cork,
on the day after the College election, he
being a candidate to reprefent that city in
parliament, and the election there demanding his immediate attendance. He had not
leifure to project the mode of infult to Mr.
Ellifon before his departure; but he paid
it off with intereft on his return : in two
days after his arrival in Dublin, and three
weeks after the election in the College,
Mr. Ellifon received a letter, figned by the
ruffian whom he had reproved, ftuffed with
the moft opprobrious epithets; he was honoured with the titles of *villanous liar* and
infamous fcoundrel. The meannefs of the
wretch, whofe fignature it bore, rendered
it unworthy of any notice ; but the ftyle
of it, the time in which it was fent, and
the Provoft's behaviour, on Mr. Ellifon's
complaint to him of this infult, evidently
proved

proved, that the Provoft himfelf had either written, or revifed and carefully correƈed it, and that it was fent by his direƈions. The Provoft's agency in this affair is ftill rendered more evident from the confideration, that no fcholar of the Houfe, let him be ever fo brutal and defperate, would have ventured to write fuch a letter to the Junior Dean, unlefs he had been well affured of proteƈion and impunity, which he knew the Provoft alone could fecure to him. Mr. Ellifon went to the Provoft, fhewed him the letter, and complained of the infult : he very coolly anfwered, that he had brought it on himfelf, and that he would not give him any fatisfaƈion for it : but in a few days after, finding that the ftory had taken wind, and that his anfwer to Mr. Ellifon was juftly confidered as an avowal that he had at leaft countenanced the bravo's infolence, if he was not the very author of the letter, he fent for him ; told him that he hoped he was not defirous of embroiling him further with the publick, and that the man fhould afk his pardon : but even this fatisfaƈion Mr. Ellifon has never fince received. Such is the treatment which has been given

to

to a clergyman, a Fellow of the College, and Junior Dean, by a *scholar*, under the auspices of the Provost! Such the manner in which the Provost supports the discipline of the College! He is not *always* so remiss in this respect; for, under the pretence of preservation of discipline, he caused a student to be publickly admonished, for no other crime, but his calling a scholar of the House, who had voted for his son, " a dirty fellow." I have been attacked myself, since I resigned my Fellowship, at the College gate, in the noon-day, by the ostensible captain of the gang, in a most outrageous manner, though I gave him no fort of provocation, and was totally unacquainted with him; and have ever since been obliged, for the protection of my life, to go armed, being under the justest apprehensions of some attempt of a fatal tendency, from the character, connexion, and behaviour of the aggressor. I shall now, as briefly as possible, give an account of Mr. Hutchinson's conduct, in respect to the Rev. Edward Berwick, a Senior Batchelor, and scholar of the House. This gentleman was a pupil of the Rev. Mr. Hales, who had been pupil to, and is the Chamber-Fellow

Fellow of the Rev. Dr. Forfayeth, whofe attachment to the Provoft's intereft I have already mentioned. His circumftances had induced him to undertake the tuition of a gentleman's fons, who refided in the country ; and, though a fcholar of the Houfe, he had been indulged with leave of abfence, from time to time, by the Board, as had been ufual before the appointment of the prefent Provoft. At the time of the annual election of fcholars of the Houfe, it had been cuftomary to inquire concerning abfent fcholars, and the caufes of their abfence ; and if it was found, that any fcholar had abfented himfelf from the College for a long courfe of time, and that it was probable he had procured fome provifion in life, which would prevent his returning to the College, and refiding therein, the Board affumed a power of depriving him of his fcholarfhip, and filling up the vacancy : this power was not ftatutable, but as it never had been exercifed but with great difcretion, and for the obvious advantage of the College, and only in the cafes of fuch perfons as had deferted the College without any intention of ever refiding, it had never been queftioned.

O   At

At the election of scholars which preceded
the laft election of members of parliament,
it had been propofed at the Board, that Mr.
Berwick fhould be deprived of his fcholarfhip for non-refidence; but the Provoft, who
at that time looked upon him as a fure voter
for his fon, thinking him to be entirely under
the influence of Dr. Forfayeth, interpofed
in his behalf; and his character being irreproachable, he was permitted to retain his
fcholarfhip. Shortly afterwards, Mr. Berwick went to the Provoft, to defire leave to
go to the country, a few days before the ex-
piration of the Trinity term in the College,
which is generally a very fhort one, and
immediately precedes the long vacation, a
time when, heretofore, no perfon whatfoever
was refufed leave of abfence. The Provoft
received him very civilly, told him he had
preferved his fcholarfhip, and recommended
his fon to his protection, his ufual method
of foliciting votes: he alfo told Mr. Berwick,
once or twice, that if he had not preferved
his fcholarfhip, it would have been given to
another perfon, *who would have voted for his
fon.* Mr. Berwick declined giving him any
direct anfwer, though he perfectly underftood

stood his meaning; and the Provost, obferving his referve, told him he would confider
of his requeft, and give him an anfwer in a
few days : after feveral applications, on all
which he was entertained by the Provoft in
the fame manner, he confulted with his
tutor, about the beft method of proceeding,
and the tutor, who, as I before obferved,
was the Provoft's creature, conftantly advifed
him to go to the Provoft, and be *explicit :*
the fagacity of an *Oedipus* was not requifite,
to enable Mr. Berwick to comprehend the
meaning of this conduct, both of his tutor
and the Provoft ; but being determined not
to engage his votes previous to the day of
election, and the duties of his tuition requiring his attendance on his pupils in the
country, he repaired thither without the
Provoft's leave, or, as the Provoft affirmed,
in contradiction to his exprefs orders. As
foon as the Provoft received notice of his
abfence, he caufed him to be cited to appear
before the Board, at a certain day, ftrongly
fufpecting that Mr. Berwick did not defign
to vote in fupport of his intereft. He caufed
another fcholar of the Houfe, the Rev. Mr.
Davoren, to be alfo cited to appear on the

O 2   fame

fame day, who had gone to the country without having afked his leave at all. The two gentlemen obeyed the citations; but though they appeared on the day appointed, he did not think fit that the affair fhould be then examined; for as it was the long vacation, he expected daily that I would defire leave of abfence, and that my place at the Board would be filled with a perfon more tractable: in this, however, I difappointed him, being refolved to ftay in town till the fate of thefe two fcholars fhould be determined; he had, befides, a further defign in this procraftination : he hoped that the dread of impending punifhment would induce the two gentlemen to promife their votes to his fon : at length, after waiting a fortnight, finding I made no movement, and the two fcholars no advances of the nature he defired, and having in the mean time, by fome extraordinary art or other, prevailed on a Member of the Board to favour his defigns, who was not before remarkable for any extraordinary attachment to him, commanding alfo the fuffrage of Dr. Forfayeth, who then was a Member of the Board, in the abfence of the Rev. Dr. Kearney, and being

thus

thus fecure of a majority, he determined to conclude the bufinefs. Though I have before fet forth the general tenor of the ftatute of abfence, yet, as Mr. Berwick's cafe came to be canvaffed before the Vifitors, it is neceffary that I fhould ftate this ftatute more accurately; it ordains, " That if any of the " Fellows or Scholars have any neceffary " caufe of departure from the College, they " fhall afk leave of abfence from the Provoft, " or, in his abfence, from the Vice-Provoft; " and, the caufe being approved, they fhall " write down their names, and the days on " which they depart, in a regifter kept for " that purpofe by the Provoft, *or, in his ab-* " *fence, by the Vice-Provoft*; and they fhall " write the days of their return in the fame " regifter, either on the days on which they " return to the College, or, at moft, the days " immediately after : but if any of the Fel- " lows or Scholars fhall omit *this*, either " through negligence or on purpofe, he fhall " for the firft omiffion be punifhed by the " *fubduction* of One Week's Commons; for " the fecond, by that of Two; for the third, " by that of Three; and for the fourth, he " fhall be punifhed at the difcretion of the

O 3 " Provoft

" Provoſt and the major part of the Senior
" Fellows." It further ordains, " That each
" Fellow ſhall be allowed ſixty-three days of
" abſence in the year, and each Scholar
" thirty-two; the year to commence on Tri-
" nity Sunday; that the Provoſt ſhall take
" care ſo to regulate the leave of abſence,
" that he ſhall never ſuffer above the third
" part of the Fellows and Scholars to be ab-
" ſent at one time, and that if any Fellow
" or Scholar ſhall abſent himſelf for a longer
" time, than that which is allotted to them
" reſpectively by the ſtatute, without having
" obtained leave of longer abſence from the
" Provoſt and Board, *he ſhall be expelled* *."
Mr. Berwick was called in firſt to the Board,
and the Provoſt charged him with having
gone to the country, not only without his
leave, but contrary to his orders, and that
his behaviour in ſo doing amounted to the
crime of Contumacy: he was then aſked,
what defence he could make. Mr. Berwick,
without either admitting or denying the
charge expreſsly, alleged, that his buſineſs
had demanded his preſence in the country,

and

---

* See the 22d chapter of the ſtatutes.

and that the narrownefs of his circumftances
had induced him to accept of the private
tuition which had been the caufe of his abfence: he was then ordered to withdraw;
and the Provoft, after informing the Board
that he had by the ftatutes the power of punifhing the crime of Contumacy by his own
fole authority, but that he had through
lenity referred the adjudication of the punifhment in this cafe to the Board, demanded
their opinions: four of the Board inftantly
voted, that Mr. Berwick fhould be deprived
of his fcholarfhip, with whom the Provoft
very readily concurred; the other three,
Drs. Clement, Murray, and I, did not concur
in the fentence: my reafons particularly for
not concurring were, 1ft, Becaufe I did not
think Mr. Berwick guilty of Contumacy,
the Provoft having, in my opinion, no power
of amplifying a fmall crime, to which a
certain punifhment is annexed by the ftatutes,
viz. the mulct of a week's commons, into
one of the greateft crimes, only by his perfo-
nally forbidding, and that too through pique
and revenge, what had been already forbidden by the ftatutes: 2dly, Becaufe, if
Mr. Berwick's crime amounted to Contu-

O 4   macy,

macy, the Board had no cognizance of the affair; and all proceedings against him before the Board were *coram non judicibus*: Contumacy being enumerated exprefsly amongft the greater crimes; in refpect to all which, the Provoft is, by the 23d chapter of the ftatutes, conftituted fole judge. 3dly, becaufe, by the faid 23d chapter, it is required, that every man, accufed of one of the greater crimes, fhall be convicted, either on his own confeffion, or by fufficient witneffes, and Mr. Berwick had not confeffed the crime, his filence on that head not amounting, in my opinion, to a confeffion, in a cafe where fo heavy a penalty as deprivation was to be inflicted, nor indeed in any criminal cafe whatfoever: befides he had not been at all urged to confefs it, the Provoft having only recited the charge to him, and afked him what defence he could make; neither had he been convicted by fufficient witneffes; for the Provoft was himfelf the only witnefs againft him, whofe fingle teftimony was not equal to that of two, and he was not a competent witnefs, for he was one, and the chief, of his judges; and ought not to

be

be both a judge and a witnefs. 4thly, becaufe, I had never known or heard, during the courfe of twenty-three years in which I had been a member of the College, that any man whatfoever had been queftion-ed about abfence in the middle of a long vacation, nor do I believe that any fuch tranfaction had ever before happened in the College fince its foundation: Which would have given me good reafon to fufpect, if I had not received pofitive proof of it, that this gentleman's crime, as well as that of Mr. Davoren, was no other than his refufing to vote at the enfuing election of members of parliament, according to the Provoft's orders. 5thly, becaufe the Pro-voft's referring this cafe to the confideration and judgment of the Board, under the mafk of lenity, feemed to me a fcheme calculated to effect two purpofes, equally unjuft and mean; the one, that he might have an opportunity of juftifying the mea-fure by the authority of the Board, and of fhifting the odium of fo extraordinary an act off his own fhoulders, upon theirs: And the other that he might be enabled to give teftimony of the fact himfelf, having

no

no other witnefs to prove it: This would
have been impoffible if he had acted as
fole judge, as by the ftatutes he ought in
refpect to Contumacy: For then he could
not have been a witnefs to prove the fact
before himfelf. But this difficulty he evaded by the ingenious device of referring the
matter to the Board, and becoming a witnefs before his fellow Judges. The idea
of his lenity in fubmitting Mr. Berwick's
cafe to the judgment of the Board, the
majority of which had already received
proper inftructions from him, is extremely
ludicrous: It is exactly of a piece with the
lenity of the inquifitors, when they deliver
over an obftinate heretick to the fecular
arm, with a mock petition, that his life
may be fpared, well knowing the faggots to
be already prepared for burning him alive.
Mr. Davoren efcaped much better: The
Provoft could not accufe him of Contumacy,
for he went to the country without afking
his leave, fo that he had no colour for
afferting that he had difobeyed his orders,
as he had not afforded him the opportunity
of giving him any. He therefore accufed
this gentleman of having abfented himfelf
for

for a longer period than thirty-two days
without leave, which is punifhable by expulfion, as I before obferved. Mr. Davoren
had gotten notice, by fome means or other,
of the charge which was to be made againft
him, previous to his appearance before the
Board; and had confulted with me about the
propereft mode of defence: I advifed him
not to admit the charge, and to give no
direct anfwer to any queftions whatfoever,
which might be propofed to him at the
Board, relative either to the times of his
departure or return, but to throw the
whole burthen of the proof on the Provoft,
which I imagined would put him to a great
difficulty; it happened as I had forefeen;
the Provoft had entirely relied on his own
ingenuity, for obtaining a confeffion from
Mr. Davoren by examination, fuppofing
him, like moft of the fcholars, but little acquainted with the ftatutes, and not thoroughly fenfible of his danger: And when
he appeared before us, the Provoft began
in the mildeft and moft infinuating manner,
to queftion him concerning the particular
time when he had departed from the College: Mr. Davoren anfwered that he had
quitted

quitted it fome time in the month of July, but did not recollect in what particular part of the month: The Provoft then, with the greateft feeming tendernefs, requefted that he would recollect himfelf, and inform him at leaft in what week of July he had left town: But Mr. Davoren's memory was entirely defective in this point; and the Provoft, having exerted all the low artifice and wheedling of an Old-Baily folicitor, to extract a confeffion from Mr. Davoren of the exact time of his departure, was entirely foiled, and obliged to content himfelf with convicting him of having gone to the country without his leave, which was punifhable only by the *fubtraction* of a week's commons. Thus Mr. Davoren, who had never afked his leave for abfenting himfelf, efcaped with a fmall punifhment, whilft Mr. Berwick, who had repeatedly, in the humbleft and moft dutiful manner, petition-ed him for leave of abfence, was punifhed with deprivation; the performance of his duty being made the handle for depriv-ing him: For if he, like Mr. Davoren, had never afked the Provoft's leave at all, the Provoft could have had no colour for
faftening

faftening the crime of Contumacy upon him.
Mr. Berwick appealed, from this fentence, to
the Vifitors of the College, who are their
graces the Primate and the Lord Arch-Bifhop
of Dublin ; and they thought proper to examine the matter publickly in the College-hall,
and reverfed the fentence. The Provoft on
this occafion conducted himfelf in the very
manner, in which his adverfaries would wifh
that he fhould behave; his clamour and
long-winded fenfelefs harangues procured
him the contempt, his infolence, malice,
and chicanery, the deteftation of the audience: he protracted the hearing, which,
from the nature of the bufinefs, ought not
to have lafted above two hours, to the
enormous length of four or five days, fix or
feven hours of each day being confumed by
it ; and of this time, though he had two
able lawyers employed in fupport of the
fentence, his own unwearied tongue employed at leaft two thirds. The Primate
thought proper to examine him and the
members of the Board upon their oaths,
relative to the fentence and the grounds of
it; and it was very remarkable, that he and
every member, who had concurred in it,
gave

gave difficrent reafons for their concurrence, and endeavoured to fupport the fentence; by different parts of the College ftatutes, no two amongft them agreeing in the caufes they affigned for voting the deprivation. The Provoft, after complaining moft tragically, (to the great amufement of the audience) that Mr. Berwick had come to him, at one time, to afk leave of abfence in very dirty boots, infifted that he had a right to produce evidence before the Vifitors, to prove that Mr. Berwick had abfented himfelf for a longer fpace of time than thirty-two days without leave, a crime, as I already mentioned, punifhable by expulfion, although he had never accufed him of that crime before the Board, but of Contumacy only in difobeying his orders; the Primate declared that the Provoft had no right to charge the appellant with any new crime before the Vifitors; that he had been accufed of a certain crime before the Board and deprived for it, and that they, the Vifitors, had come there, upon his petition of appeal, to inquire whether he had been ftatutably convicted of, and expelled for, that crime; and not to try him for a new crime, of which he had not

been

been before accufed, and which was properly
cognizable, in the firft inftance, before the
Board: the Provoft then exclaimed, that
he was not fuffered to produce his evidence,
and poured forth fuch a torrent of declama-
tory nonfenfe, that the Primate, wearied out,
thought it would be the beft method of
fhortening the bufinefs, to permit him to
produce what evidence he pleafed ; and he
accordingly produced one Mr. Mofs, a Clergyman, married to his wife's fifter, to prove
that he had feen Mr. Berwick, at thirty miles
diftance from Dublin, on a certain day previous to that alleged by him to be the day
of his departure; and alfo Mr. Berwick's
tutor, to prove, from fome private confiden-
tial difcourfe between him and his pupil,
relative to his beft method of procuring
leave of abfence; that it was probable he
had gone to the country earlier, than he was
willing to admit: this laft gentleman's conduct, in giving evidence on fuch a point
againft his pupil, is juft as proper, as if an
attorney or counfel fhould give evidence
againft their client, in refpect to the fecrets
intrufted to them by him, in the courfe of
bufinefs; and an objection on this ground
having

having been made to his evidence, the Provoft endeavoured to fupport it, by reciting
the following claufe in the oath of a Fellow,
" I will to the beft of my power defend and
" preferve the fafety, dignity, peace, and
" advantage of the College and of all the
" Students in it, particularly of the Provoft
" and the fenior Fellows;" as if the betray-
ing the fecrets neceffarily intrufted by his
pupil to him, for the purpofe of confirming
his pupils unftatutable deprivation, tended
to the defence or procurement of the fafety,
dignity, peace, and advantage of the College,
the Provoft and the fenior Fellows; and did
not trench upon the fafety, dignity, peace,
and advantage of his pupil, which he was
bound by the fame oath to defend and procure. The Provoft's lawyers endeavoured
to fupport the fentence, by obferving, that
Mr. Berwick had been in danger of deprivation for abfence previous to the laft Trinity
Sunday; that his repeating the offence fo
foon after was a confiderable aggravation;
that the word, *this*, in the claufe of the
ftatute of abfence, which ordains, " That if
" any of the Fellows or Scholars fhall omit
" *this*, either through negligence or on pur-
" pofe,

" pofe, he fhall for 'the firft omiffion be
" punifhed by the fubtraction of one week's
" commons, &c." ought to refer only to that
part of the preceding claufe, which relates
to the entrance of the names of fuch as
return in the Provoft's regifter, and not to
the whole preceding claufe, that therefore
no exprefs punifhment is annexed in the
ftatute of abfence to the omiffion of the
performance of the duties enjoined by the
firft part of the claufe, fuch as afking the
Provoft leave of abfence, &c. but the punifhment of the breaches of fuch duty is left to
the difcretion of the Provoft and fenior
Fellows: that if the word *this* fhould be
underftood to refer to the whole preceding
claufe, the Provoft would be difabled from
doing that part of his duty, which confifts
in his compelling two thirds of the Fellows
and fcholars to refide always in the College;
the punifhment for departing from the
College without his leave, if fuch a conftruction fhould prevail, not being fufficient
to deter the members of the College from
committing fuch tranfgreffions; that Mr.
Berwick's crime was greater, than that of
going to the country without the Provoft's
P permiffion;

permiffion; for he had gone to the country
in oppofition to the Provoft's commands,
and was therefore guilty of a breach of his
oath, by which he fwears to obey the Provoft moft willingly in all things lawful and
honeft; that in the 10th chapter of the ftatutes it is ordained, that if any Fellow, appointed a tutor to any ftudent by the Provoft, fhall refufe to accept the charge, he
fhall incur the punifhment of the crime of
contempt againft the government or difcipline of the College, and fhall be punifhed
according to the difcretion of the Provoft
and the major part of the feven fenior
Fellows; that Mr. Berwick's crime was fuch
a contempt, and was therefore properly cognizable by the Provoft and Board, and punifhable according to their difcretion; and
finally that it had been proved in this cafe,
that Mr. Berwick had remained abfent from
the College longer than the term of thirty-
two days without leave, the punifhment of
which tranfgreffion, by the ftatutes, was expulfion, and that the examination of fuch a
fact came properly before their Graces on
this appeal, who were competent judges of,
and ought to award the ftatutable punifhment

to

to fuch a tranfgreffion. It was anfwered by the counfel on behalf of the appellant, that Mr. Berwick, even by the confeffion of fome of the fenior Fellows, who had voted for his deprivation, was a man of moft irreproachable charaĉer; that it had been always cuſtomary to grant confiderable indulgencies in the College to fuch men; that the danger of deprivation, which Mr. Berwick had incurred before Trinity Sunday, arofe more from a cuſtom eftablifhed in the College, for the purpofe of accommodating as many deferving candidates as poffible with fcholarfhips, than from any crime committed by him, which would warrant deprivation; that the power of deprivation, affumed by the Board on fuch occafions, was not ftatutable, (the ftatutes ordaining a gradation of punifhments previous to deprivation for abfence) but had been connived at and acquiefced in, becaufe it had always heretoforebeen exercifed for the emolument of the College, the fcholarfhips vacated, on fuch occafions, being immediately filled up by deferving candidates, the vacancies being declared, and the fcholars eleĉed at one and the fame time: whereas, in the prefent cafe,

if

if the deprivation fhould be confidered as valid, the fcholarfhip muft remain vacant near eleven months (that being the diftance of time between the deprivation and next election of fcholars) to the injury of the College : that a deprivation of any fcholar for abfence, at fuch a feafon of the year, had never been before heard of in the College, and that an unftatutable cuftom winked at, when exerted only for the advantage of the College, ought to be fuppreffed, when made a cloak and pretence for injuring the College, as well as individuals. That if Mr. Berwick had committed any ftatutable crime, by ab-fenting himfelf from the College previous to Trinity Sunday, as he had been abfolved from fuch crime by the Board, who agreed to permit him to retain his fcholarfhip, it ought not now to be alleged againft him by way of aggravation of any offence which he might have been guilty of, in point of abfence fince, as it is exprefsly provided by the ftatutes, that all abfences, both of Fellows and fcholars, fhall be computed from Trinity Sunday annually. That the word *this*, in the claufe of the ftatute of abfence, naturally refers to the whole pre-ceding claufe, and not to a part of it, and that

that therefore the punifhment prefcribed by the ftatute, for the firft offence in quitting the College without the Provoft's leave, is only the *fubtraction* of a week's commons; that the argument brought to fupport this forced and unnatural conftruction of the ftatute, that the word *this* fhould refer only to one part of the preceding fentence, and not to the whole, to wit, that if it fhould be taken to refer to the whole, the Provoft would not be able to do his duty in retaining two thirds of the Fellows and fcholars in the College at all times, is abfurd on the very face of it, for as every Fellow is allowed but fixty-three days of abfence in the whole year, and every fcholar but thirty-two, both being liable to expulfion for any longer abfence, and as departing from the College without the Pro-voft's leave, at any time, is punifhable by the ftatute, it is evident that the Provoft, by the exertion of his ftatutable authority only, might always command the attendance in the College of more than two thirds of the Fellows and fcholars, if he thought proper to do fo. That Mr. Berwick had committed no greater nor other offence, than that of quit-ting the College, in the firft inftance, without

obtaining

obtaining leave of abfence from the Provoft, and that therefore no greater nor other punifhment fhould have been inflicted on him, than the fubtraction of a week's commons; that the Provoft's commanding or forbidding any thing, already commanded or forbidden by the ftatutes, could not make the tranfgreffors of the ftatutes, in fuch points, liable to heavier punifhments than the ftatutes had ordained : becaufe the authority of the ftatutes is much higher than that of the Provoft, and they contain the rules prefcribed for the conduct of each member of the College, and define the punifhments for the violation of each rule, according to the wills of the royal Founders. That there was no neceffity for rummaging the ftatutes to find out crimes, with heavy punifhments annexed, for the purpofes of moulding Mr. Berwick's offence, already accurately defined by the ftatutes, into a likenefs of any crime the Board thought proper to fix upon in that code, and of fubjecting him by fuch means to a heavy punifhment for a flight offence. That the ftatutes were as fevere and rigorous as they could be framed, and therefore ought not to be ftretched beyond their limits. That the

Provoft's

Provoft's charge of a breach of oath againft a fcholar, who tranfgreffed a ftatute in which a punifhment is defined for the tranfgreffion, merely becaufe he has thought fit to give his commands in affirmance of the ftatute, is of moft dangerous confequence; perjury being a crime, for which the ftatutes ordain the moft capital academick punifhment, and the Provoft, by the ingenious device of commanding a member of the College not to commit a tranfgreffion, the ftatutable punifhment of which, is no more than a fine of two pence, might contrive to ex- pel him, if he fhould at any time inad- vertently commit the tranfgreffion, and thus punifh the flighteft fault with the heavieft punifhment, which would render every man's freehold in the College total- ly infecure, and tenable only at the pleafure of the Provoft. That their Graces had come to the College, on the appeal of Mr. Berwick, merely to inquire into, and re- drefs a grievance complained of, by virtue of a power incident to the office of vifitors by the common law: that their bufinefs was to inquire what crime the appellant had been charged with, what proof had

been

been made of his having committed it, and,
if it fhould be their opinion that the crime
had been fully proved, or confeffed, to
confider whether the punifhment inflicted
on him was the ftatutable punifhment prefcribed for fuch crime: but that it was no
part of the bufinefs of their Graces, to inquire into any other crimes which the Provoft might think proper to charge upon
the appellant, with which he had never
been charged before, and which were but
feeble fupporters of a rotten caufe, totter-
ing under the preffure of its own iniquity:
that therefore the evidence of Mr. Mofs,
and the appellant's tutor, was no way rele-
vant in the matter before their Graces, and
was befides totally infufficient to prove the
allegation of the Provoft, that Mr. Berwick
had abfented himfelf from the College for
a longer period than thirty-two days. When
the Vifitors delivered their opinions, the
Primate entered at large into the matter,
he ftated and refuted, with great accuracy
and concifenefs, every thing advanced in
fupport of the deprivation, either by the
Provoft or his Counfel, which bore even
the femblance of argument; and difplayed

fuch

such sagacity and knowledge of law in this matter, such elegance and dignity in his manner, as astonished and delighted the whole audience (the Provost and his adherents excepted.) The Arch-Bishop of Dublin concurred fully with the Primate, and therefore spoke very shortly; but, as it would seem by way of consoling the Provost on his defeat, and in some measure to skreen him from the contempt of the Students, which his behaviour in this affair had so justly earned, he pronounced a sort of eulogium on him: as this commendation came from so great an authority, and contained compliments to the Provost so unmerited, that it is plain he had found means to deceive his Grace in some particulars; and as he has not failed to make use of it by way of justification of his conduct, I hope I shall not be considered as deviating in any shape from the profound respect, which I entertain for his Grace of Dublin, if I examine how far the Provost's behaviour entitled him to these compliments from him. During the whole time of the hearing of this appeal, the Provost's rage had so far overpowered what little understand-

ing

ing he had, that he behaved with much infolence to the Primate. As this great Prelate had always expreffed his difapprobation of his appointment to the Provoftfhip, well knowing how fatal a blow it was to the church of Ireland, over which his Grace has long prefided, and watched, with the tender anxiety of a father, and the piety of a true chriftian bifhop ; and as a man, confpicuous, like his Grace, for the conftant practice of every virtue, muft be naturally an object of hatred to perfons of an oppofite character, the Provoft had conceived an inveterate diflike of the Primate. This temper of mind, aided by his natural petulance and folly, and inflamed by the profpect of impending difgrace, caufed him to overleap all bounds of prudence and decency on this occafion, in refpect to the Primate ; but as he well knew that his infolence was punifhable, even with deprivation, by the Vifitors, if they fhould concur in opinion, he took the precaution of paying many compliments to the Arch-Bifhop of Dublin, during the courfe of the hearing, and made feveral little mean attempts, and exerted fome low cunning, to

excite

excite diſſention between the two Viſitors: this artifice was ineffectual; he had
men of abilities to deal with; the Primate
behaved with a patience, dignity, and ſpirit, which cauſed all the ſhafts of the Provoſt's malice to recoil upon himſelf. This
diſappointment only whetted his rancour:
in a ſhort time after the hearing of the appeal, a pamphlet was publiſhed, entitled
" an examination of the Viſitors conduct
" upon the hearing the Rev. Edward Ber-
" wick's appeal in the hall of Trinity Col-
" lege, Dublin." The ſtyle was barbarous,
and it contained almoſt as many lies as
lines, infallible marks of the author! many things in it were ludicrous; ſuch as,
calling the Attorney General the Provoſt's
rival: it being full as proper, to call Sir
Iſaac Newton, the rival of Partridge the al-
manack maker: many abſurd; ſuch as ſty-
ling the Provoſt the head of the Univerſity *.
The whole contained the moſt virulent abuſe
of the Primate; but one aſſertion, which is
frequently repeated in it, deſerves ſome ani-
madverſion :

* His Royal Highneſs, the Duke of Gloucefter, is head of the
Univerſity, being the Chancellor; Mr. Hutchinſon, as an
honorary Doctor, is no member whatſoever of the Univerſity.

madverfion: as almoft every perfon, who
had heard of Mr. Berwick's deprivation,
well knew that the Provoft had caufed him
to be deprived, merely becaufe he would not
promife to vote for his fon on the election,
the author of the pamphlet thought fit to
turn the tables on the Provoft's adverfaries,
or fuch as he thought to be fo, and,
therefore, moft falfely afferted, that the
Primate reftored Mr. Berwick, with the
view of affifting the Attorney general in
his election: now the fact is, that Mr,
Berwick had not promifed to vote for the
Attorney general, previous to his refto-
ration ; neither had he been ever folicited
by the Attorney general, or any of his friends,
to vote for him, before that period. And
the Provoft, to demonftrate to the world
the caufe for which he had deprived Mr.
Berwick, thought fit to reject his vote at the
election, although he complied with the
fentence of the Vifitors, in reftoring him to
the full emoluments of his fcholarfhip; thus
admitting him to be a fcholar in all things,
except where it clafhed with his own private
intereft, and militated againft the project,
in the execution of which he had originally
caufed him to be deprived. His excufe for
                                    acting

acting in this flagrant manner on the election, where he was the returning officer, and sworn to the due execution of his duty, is, that the restoration of Mr. Berwick, by the sentence of the Visitors, is not valid without the approbation * of the Chancellor, altho' no

* The Visitors of the College, by Charter, are the Chancellor of the University, or, in his absence, the Vice-chancellor, (who at present is the Primate) and the Arch-bishop of Dublin. There is a clause in that part of the Charter of Charles, which defines the duty of Visitors, to the following effect : " If the "Vice-chancellor of the University and the Arch-bishop of " Dublin should disagree upon any point, and in all the more " weighty affairs of the College, nothing shall ever be done " without the approbation of the Chancellor, or if any thing " be done, it shall be void." The meaning of this clause in the Charter is more fully explained in the 27th chapter of the Statutes ; where, after the duty of the Visitors in their *triennial visitation*, and their power of depriving the Provost, or any member of the College, are fully set forth, there is the following provision : " Always provided, according to the tenor of " the Charter, that neither in *deprivations*, nor in any of the " more weighty affairs of the College, any thing shall be ever " done, without the approbation of the Chancellor (whom we " appoint the Chief Visitor), or if any thing be so done, it shall " be void." The Provost, from these two clauses, insists, that the restoration of Mr. Berwick, by the sentence of the Visitors, is not valid, until the Chancellor approves of it. But it is to be observed, that the Chancellor, when absent, is not a Visitor, as may be proved from the Charter, and that therefore the two Arch-bishops were the only statutable visitors in this case ; that they acted by virtue of the power incident to their office by the
Common

no point of law is settled more immovably,
than that the sentence of Visitors, in redressing grievances, is final and conclusive,
as may be seen in the case of Philips and
Bury, in Lord Raymond's Reports, and in
Shower's Parliamentary Cases : and though
he himself admitted it to be so, by restoring
Mr. Berwick immediately to all the emoluments of his scholarship. But as this point
will soon be debated before a court of law,
I shall say no more concerning it. The
pamphlet

Common Law of the realm, in *redressing a grievance*; and that
(unless in cases where this their power from the Common Law
is expresly restrained by the Charter and Statutes) their adjudication is final and conclusive, as may be proved from the learning
in the case of Philips and Bury : now this part of their power,
with which they are invested by the Common Law, is not at all
abridged by either the Charter or Statutes, but only their power
in their *triennial visitation* ; which, if exerted in Deprivation,
or in any very weighty business of the College, is by the Statutes
subjected to the control of the Chancellor. By the word
deprivations in the Statute, are meant Deprivations by the
Visitors in their triennial visitation : in Berwick's case the Visitors did not deprive in a triennial visitation, or at all ; they only
restored by virtue of their authority derived from the Common
Law. It is further to be observed, that the Expulsion of a
Member has never been held one of the more weighty affairs of
the College, on which the Chancellor is to be consulted, being
frequently performed by the Provost and Fellows, without con-
sulting either with the Chancellor or Visitors ; and Expulsion is
an affair, at least, as weighty and worthy of the review of the
Chancellor, as Restoration.

pamphlet concluded with reciting the Arch-
bifhop of Dublin's panegyrick on the Provoſt,
which, as there ſet forth, contained a commendation of his plans, with reſpeĉt to the
improvement of the buildings of the College,
his munificence in founding two profeſſor-
ſhips of modern languages, and his regulations for the improvement of literature.
His merits, in theſe particulars, I ſhall, therefore, now proceed to inquire into, although
the reader may make a pretty juſt eſtimate
of them, by what I have already ſtated. In
reſpeĉt to his plans for improving the buildings of the College, it is to be obſerved, that
none of them have ever yet been executed,
or even begun, and that he has prevented
the erecĉtion of a plain brick building, abſolutely neceſſary for the accommodation of
the ſtudents, to the infinite detriment of the
College; and that he cannot arrogate to himfelf the merit of any future improvements in
the buildings of the College, ſuch improvements having been projecĉted long before he
became Provoſt, and the parliament having
granted large ſums for re-building the College; £12,000 of which (as before mentioned)
are yet unexpended: he has, indeed, procured

cured the fum of £2,500 from the Board of Erafmus Smith, for the purpofe of erecting a theatre in the College; but the College being already furnifhed with an elegant fenate-houfe, this theatre has been looked upon as ufelefs, and the money is to be laid out in erecting a new hall. Whatever merit he may claim from this fervice to the College, certainly it cannot be equal to that of the late Provoft, who procured infinitely larger fums from the fame Board, and applied them to ufeful purpofes in the College; to wit, to the promotion and encouragement of the fciences; he never conceived the idea of fquandering them on *gewgaws*; befides, Mr. Hutchinfon has quartered one of his dependants on the College, as an architect, with an annual falary of £150, which amounts to the legal intereft of the fum he procured. His munificence, in founding two Profefforfhips of Modern Languages, amounts to this: he has imported two foreigners, and affigned them chambers in the College, (notwithftanding the fcarcity of lodgings) to teach the French, German, Italian, and Spanifh Languages, to fuch ftudents as choofe to become their pupils; and

and pay them for their inftructions: he declared, that he engaged to pay each of thefe
men £100 yearly, but he charged the College with all their travelling expenfes. Thefe
two language-mafters he calls Profeffors, in
the true ftyle of fchool-mafters, who generally, in Dublin, call their fchools Acade-
mies; and he has lately taken care to eafe
himfelf of the obligation to pay their ftipends,
having procured an annual allowance from
government for that purpofe. This is the
foundation of two new Profefforfhips of
Modern Languages! Profefforfhips of modern languages being eftablifhed in the
Univerfities in England, and a menage in
that of Oxford, he thought he might drown
the publick clamour, excited by his extraordinary promotion, in the eclat of intro-
ducing fimilar eftablifhments here: the erection of a Riding-houfe he recommended
with great earneftnefs to the Board, and
the endowment of a Profeffor of Horfeman-
fhip, but without fuccefs: any perfon, who
will confider the different fituations of the
College of Dublin and the Univerfities of
Oxford and Cambridge, will eafily perceive

Q   that

that fuch inftitutions, though ufeful in the Englifh Seminaries, are totally unneceffary here. This College is fituated almoft in the middle of a city, the largeft in Chriftendom, except London and Paris; every ftudent, defirous of acquiring the polite accomplifh- ments, can readily procure inftructors in the city; they may be taught fencing, dancing, and the modern languages, in their cham- bers, on very reafonable terms, and there is a menage in the Caftle of Dublin, within a quarter of a mile of the College, open for the inftruction of all gentlemen in horfe- manfhip, at a very moderate expenfe: the Univerfities of Oxford and Cambridge are both fituated in country towns, which, ab- ftracted from the Univerfities, are fmall and inconfiderable; they are not furnifhed with proper inftructors in thofe accomplifhments which I have juft mentioned, and, therefore, it became, in fome fort, neceffary for the governors of thefe feminaries to found aca- demick eftablifhments for the inftruction of the young gentlemen, committed to their care, in thefe particulars: thus the different fituations of thefe feminaries render the fame

eftablifhments

establishments necessary and laudable in the English, absurd and useless in the Irish, and, perhaps, even pernicious; as teachers of modern languages, fencing and dancing masters, and horse-riders, are not always the most eligible companions for youth, and therefore ought not, unless from necessity, to be suffered to take up their residence amongst the students. Experience has demonstrated the inutility of these language-masters in the College of Dublin; for though they have been settled there above two years, they have not yet been honoured with any considerable number of pupils; perhaps it is rather an exaggeration to assert, that about five, out of five hundred students, have applied to them for instruction. The last head of the Archbishop's praise, of Mr. Hutchinson, contained advantageous expressions of his new regulations, for the improvement of literature: and whatever pains had been taken by the Provost, and his agents, to deceive his Grace, in respect to the plans of College buildings, and foundation of new professorships, they must certainly have exerted the powers of falsehood and misrepresentation, with more

than

than ordinary activity and impudence, to induce his Grace to believe, that a perfon fo very illiterate, as I have already proved Mr. Hutchinfon to be, could in any manner improve the courfe of education adopted and eftablifhed in the College of Dublin, when he was appointed Provoft. His vanity and ignorance certainly prompted him, on his advancement, to find fault with every thing he did not underftand, that is, with the whole circle of the fciences, and the method in which they were taught in the College : he was poffeffed with a fort of rage for alteration, he had a paffion for being efteemed learned, and imagined that he might procure the reputation of being a fcholar, by interfering in, and new modelling learned inftitutions : he was convinced, from experience, that, in moft profeffions, external appearance and artful management were fufficient fubftitutes for real merit, and procured a man the reputation of it. Preparative to each of the quarterly examinations, the ftudents are obliged to read certain of the Greek and Latin clafficks ; I have already ftated the ridiculous and pernicious alterations

tions he has made in this claffical part of
College education; to give one inftance, out
of many, of the abfurdity of his new regulations in this particular, he has fubftituted
the jejune, puerile, ftyle of Juftin, in place
of the elegant latinity of Cæfar's Commen-
taries: fuch injudicious alterations as thefe,
only lightly mifchievous, becaufe they are
not very important, with fome unftatutable
orders, iffued by his own authority, concerning attendance at the preleƈtions of the
Profeffors, are the only regulations whatfoever he has made, any way relating to literature; and how far they tend to its improvement, let the reader determine.

I fhall now proceed to that part of my
fubjeƈt, which relates to his behaviour to me,
whilft I was a Member of the College. I fhall
ftate the faƈts truly, abftaining as much as
poffible from any remarks upon them:
indeed I would have very willingly omitted
any account of them at all; but as I had
the peculiar honour to be marked out by
him as the principal objeƈt of his malice,
and as his conduƈt to me is therefore diftin-

Q 3   guifhed

guifhed by the ftrongeft features of malignant
cunning and revenge, I think a true portrait
of it will give the publick a jufter idea of
the ruin impending over the College, than
any of the circumftances which I have already
related. I fcorn to appeal to the publick,
with a view of procuring redrefs or fatisfaction, for any private injury which I may
have fuftained by him; being perfectly
convinced, that I am able to procure them
for myfelf, at any time I may think
proper, by other arms than my pen: my
only objects are, to imprefs the world
with a true notion of the facrifice which
has been made, to glut the avarice of
Mr. Hutchinfon, and to convince the publick, that the ruin of the College, and the
confequent irreparable damage of this kingdom, will be the certain effects of his promotion, if he is fuffered to remain for any
length of time in his prefent ftation. In
the execution of this defign, to which I have
been prompted by no private views whatfoever, it has become neceffary for me to re-
veal the enormity of his oppreffions in the
College,

College, and I therefore cannot omit the detail of his unjuft attacks on me, whilft I continued a Fellow : as they are, at leaft, of as malignant a nature, as any of his attempts there, and as expreffive of his temper and defigns. He began his injurious behaviour to me, by a grofs infult which he threw upon me, without the leaft provocation being given on my part, and on the following remarkable occafion. In the oath, which every man who is elected a Fellow is obliged to take, there is the following claufe. "I alfo profefs that I do not now "poffefs any ecclefiaftical benefice whatfo-"ever, nor will I accept of any, fo long "as I fhall continue a Fellow of this Col-"lege, unlefs it be in the city of Dublin, "or in places within fifteen miles of the "city, if it be a benefice with cure of "fouls; or if it be not a benefice with "cure of fouls, within the diftance of "thirty miles at moft, but in neither cafes "exceeding the value of ten pounds fterling, "in the book of rates in the King's ex-"chequer." The Provoft, from the moment of his appointment, had determined

to

to exert all his influence to fecure the election of two of his creatures as reprefentatives of the College in parliament, and
quickly perceiving that the tutors, having
great intereft with their pupils, could, of
all the members of the College, moft effectually ferve his electioneering defigns, he
refolved to reconcile fome of thefe to his
views, by every means in his power. The
Rev. Mr. Hales had, at the time of his
appointment, the moft numerous lift of
pupils in the College; he lived in the fame
chambers with, and was totally under the
guidance and direction of, the Rev. Doctor
Forfayeth, who had been his tutor, and
was a fort of patron to him. A church
living in the gift of the crown, of about
three hundred pounds yearly value, became
vacant; and the Provoft determined to
attach Doctor Forfayeth to his intereft,
by procuring this living for him : unluckily for Doctor Forfayeth, this benefice
confifted of a number of fmall livings uni-
ted, and had the cure of fouls; fome of
the livings were within fifteen miles of
Dublin, fome of them far beyond this limit.
The

The value of them all together, in the book of rates in the Kings exchequer, amounted to about eighteen pounds per annum. Thefe bars to the acceptance of fuch a living may feem *infurmountable*, by a Fellow of this College, to a perfon who has read the oath of a Fellow; but Doctor Forfayeth found no difficulty in bounding over them with the help of the Provoft, who eafily procured the Lord Lieutenant's promife to prefent, and the Doctor's confent to accept: but the Doctor had ftill one fmall fcruple, which the Provoft undertook to remove; as the duration of human life is uncertain, the Doctor apprehended that a future Provoft might, perhaps, not interpret the Fellow's oath in the fame favourable fenfe for him, as the prefent Provoft: and he could not bear the thought of refigning, or lofing his Fellowfhip: it was therefore refolved by thefe two friends, that the circumftances of the living fhould be explained to the Board, and that the Provoft, by the force of his eloquence, fhould demonftrate to them the propriety of Doctor Forfayeth's accepting this living, and retaining his Fellowfhip, lowſhip, notwithſtanding his oath : this was certainly a difficult taſk for a mathematician, being of the ſame nature with proving, that two added to two make only three; but it was eaſy for an orator; particularly when that orator was the almoſt deſpotick governor of his auditors : and the Provoſt undertook to procure the Board, not only to approve of the Doctor's accepting the living, but to enter their approbation in the College regiſtry, which would be a ſhield to defend the Doctor againſt the attacks of any future ſcrupulous Provoſt, on the ſcore of his oath. The Board was accordingly aſſembled, and both Doctor Forfayeth and I were members of it; two ſenior Fellows being abſent. Doctor Forfayeth produced to us a caſe, in which the circumſtances of the living were ſtated, and a paper, in the form of a letter, detached from the caſe, ſubſcribed by a civilian of rank and merit, with whom he had an intimacy : this paper contained a ſort of opinion or argument, tending to juſtify the Doctor's acceptance of the living; but it plainly appeared on the face of the opinion, that

that it was not given upon the cafe produced to us, nor was the cafe, upon which
the opinion was given, at all ſhewn to us.
To prove that the living was within the
limits preſcribed by the oath, the Doctor
produced a compaſs, and an old map of the
province of Leinſter by Sir William Petty;
and endeavoured to ſhew, that the remoteſt
church (for there were two upon the benefice) was juſt fifteen miles from Dublin, in
a ſtraight or bird-line : even this part of the
farce required a dextrous management of
the dividers, in which the Doctor ſeemed
to be very expert. The Provoſt then, according to cuſtom, made a tedious harangue,
praiſing the Doctor's ſtrict attention to the
obligation of his oath, blaming, however,
his ſcrupulouſneſs on this occaſion, in ſo
clear a cafe, telling us of the nature, uſe,
and adoption of bird-lines, in the room of
zig zags &c. &c. &c. I had never before
heard of this buſineſs, but as I was, at the
time, profeſſor of civil law, in the Univerſity, and as the opinion of the Board was
required upon the cafe, I thought it became
my profeſſion and ſtation, to pay ſome attention

tention to it : and whilſt the Provoſt was haranguing, I read the caſe and opinion very carefully. It did not require much attention to form an opinion on the caſe ; but as my thoughts upon it were very different from thoſe of the civilian before mentioned, for whom I had a great reſpect, and alſo from thoſe expreſſed by the Provoſt, I determined to deliver them with all deference and humility, and in as brief a manner as poſſible. I accordingly obſerved, that I did not think the opinion before us was founded on legal principles, and mentioned one, on which the whole ſeemed to be built, which I apprehended not to be law; and that I did not think any Fellow of the College could, conſcientiouſly, accept of an eccleſiaſtical benefice, circumſtanced as the living in queſtion, and retain his Fellowſhip. The Provoſt had ſcarce patience to hear me expreſs theſe few words : he flew into a violent rage; reproved me in the harſheſt terms, ſcarcely refraining from downright abuſe, and behaved to me in ſo indecent and outrageous a manner, that all preſent were ſtruck with aſtoniſhment. I was fully ſenſible of the indignity with which I was treated, but

recollecting

recollecting my fituation to be the fame,
with that of a man bound hand and foot,
lying at the feet of a ruffian brandifhing a
fword over him, I behaved with calmnefs
and filence, till the firft ebullitions of his
wrath had evaporated : I then obferved, that
it was far from my intentions to give any
offence to the Provoft, or to any perfon ; that
I was only delivering my opinion, in the
courfe of my duty, upon a point fubmitted
to the confideration of the Board, of which I
was a member, by the Provoft himfelf ; that
it was a point too in which the Board had
no concern whatfoever ; that the Board were
not the patrons of the living, and that no
perfon there was concerned in the matter,
except Doctor Forfayeth, whofe confcience
would inform him better than lawyers, civilians, or the Board, what line of conduct
he ought to follow on the occafion ; even
this apology for my opinion did not fatisfy
the Provoft ; I underwent a fecond furious
rebuke ; and Doctor Forfayeth openly declaring that his confcience was perfectly
fatisfied, and that he would accept the
living, the Board (partly intimidated, as I
believe,

believe, by the treatment which they had
feen me receive) agreed to enter a fort of
approbation of Doctor Forfayeth's acceptance of the living, on the College regiftry;
inferting, however, the cafe and opinion
produced by the Doctor, as the juftification
of this extorted approbation, and referring to
them. It is worthy to be remarked, that
Doctor Forfayeth did not accept the living
for three or four months after this tranfaction: the circumftances of the living, and
the Provoft's behaviour to me, became a fubject of converfation in the College and the
city; and though the Doctor had declared at
the Board, that his confcience was perfectly
fatisfied, and that he would accept the
living, yet, in the interval between this
tranfaction and his acceptance of it, he has
fince declared, that he applied for, and
obtained the opinions of three * or four very
eminent

* I have been informed that thefe gentlemen have attempted
the Doctor's juftification, in the point of diftance, by computed
miles, bird-lines, unions, &c. in the point of value, by palliated
unions, &c. I have never been able to procure a fight of thefe
opinions, or the cafes upon which they have been given; but

as

eminent lawyers and civilians, and that
they have all agreed, that he might retain
his Fellowſhip, and accept the living, without breaking through the obligations of his
oath. Theſe opinions he and his friends
have often promiſed to publiſh, but have
hitherto declined it. One thing, however,
is plain from his conduct in this reſpect;
that he did not procure theſe laſt mentioned
opinions in order to ſatisfy his conſcience,
but merely for defence. At the time this
affair happened, Mr. Hutchinſon had not
ſpoken to me about my votes at the elec-.
tion : when he had time to reflect on the

as they have been repreſented to me, his juſtification, in point of
diſtance, deſtroys his juſtification in point of value, and *vice
verſâ*. Though I have a very great reſpect for the gentlemen,
who are ſaid to have given their opinions on theſe points, and
know them to be men of very great abilities, yet I will undertake to ſupport the opinion I delivered at the Board, upon the
caſe ſtated by Doctor Forſayeth himſelf, now on record in the
College regiſtry ; and to prove in print (provided the caſes ſaid
to be ſtated, and the opinions ſaid to be obtained by Doctor
Forſayeth, ſhall be printed) that no Fellow of the College of
Dublin can conſcientiouſly accept of a living, circumſtanced as
the living in queſtion, whilſt he remains a Fellow, either in
reſpect to the value or diſtance ; notwithſtanding all the chicane
of computed miles, bird-lines, palliated unions, &c. &c.

indecency

indecency of his behaviour to me, he began, as I suppose, to be afraid, that my resentment might induce me to vote against his interest, and in order to obviate the effects of any distaste I might have conceived, by a sudden application, he sent for me the very next day, and asked, or rather demanded, a promise of my two votes for any persons he should think proper to nominate: I told him that his Majesty's Attorney general, from repeated favours conferred upon me, had a right to every attention and duty I could pay him, on the principles of gratitude: that I had the honour and advantage of the protection and countenance of that great man, long before I had even suspected that Mr. Hutchinson would ever be Provost of the College: that if I had been bound by the same ties to him, he would have good reason to think me a very worthless person, if I deserted his interest: that I did not intend to give the Attorney general any reason to entertain a bad opinion of me, and that my votes and whatever interest I had, should be exerted in support of the

Attorney

attorney on the enfuing election : he affected
to be much furprifed, and endeavoured to
faften a promife upon me of one vote at leaft,
from fome vague converfation, which had
formerly happened between him and me :
but I told him, that, till that inftant, I had
never the leaft difcourfe with him, concerning elections, and that if he underftood any
compliments which I might have paid him,
in the ufual courfe of converfation, as any
way relating to fervices to be performed for
him on an election, he had been greatly miftaken : on this he difmiffed me, not without
evident marks of his difpleafure and difappointment. At this time, I ftood indebted
to the College, in the fum of £300 or
thereabouts : this debt had been contracted
partly in purchafing chambers, when I had
been firft elected a Fellow (Fellows in the
College of Dublin being obliged to buy their
chambers) partly by the expenfe in which
my neceffary refidence at the Temple, in the
ftudy of my profeffion, had involved me : I
had been originally compelled to enter into
the profeffion of the law, by the ftatutes, on
the refignation of his Fellowfhip by the late
Dr. Sullivan ; the Junior Mafter of Arts,

R   among

among the Fellows, which I then was, being
obliged to apply himſelf to the ſtudy of that
profeſſion, on the death or reſignation of the
Law-fellow : the perſon thus deſtined to
the profeſſion of the law, unleſs he has ſome
private fortune (which was not my caſe) is
put to great inconvenience ; and his Fellowſhip is much leſs lucrative than that of any
other Fellow : for the Junior Fellows here
are very ſlenderly provided for by the College; their income generally amounting to
£60 per ann. excluſive of their commons :
their greateſt profits ariſe from their pupils,
but the Law-fellow cannot ſtudy and exerciſe
his profeſſion, and attend pupils at the ſame
time ; the duties are abſolutely incompatible:
thus the Law-fellow is laid under a neceſſity
of dedicating himſelf to a profeſſion, expen-
ſive in the acquiſition, unprofitable in the
practice, for ſome years at leaſt ; and at the
ſame time of foregoing all the advantages
ariſing from pupilage, the chief ſupport of a
Junior Fellow, with a very ſcanty fund for his
ſubſiſtence : The reader may from hence
perceive, that my College debt was contracted from neceſſity; and it was alſo
much leſs than the College-debts of a
great majority of the Fellows, who were
under

under no fuch neceffity of contracting
them. I might be at this time reafonably
accounted the next in fucceffion to a Senior Fellowfhip; for Dr. Dabzack, my immediate Senior, was, in the courfe of a few
months afterwards, to fucceed to a Senior
Fellowfhip, on the refignation of one of the
Senior Fellows, who was to be promoted to
a valuable living, then vacant, in the gift of
the College; and the emoluments of a Senior Fellowfhip would, in one half year,
pay my debt; befides my chambers and effects in the College were nearly fufficient to
pay it, in cafe of my death, before I became a Senior Fellow. Thefe confiderations
had hitherto prevented the College from giving me any trouble about this matter; my falary was regularly paid to me; and the Provoft and board had been content to wait until
it was convenient for me to difcharge the
debt: In this I was treated with no peculiar
favour; the fame indulgence was extended
to all the Fellows: it was the cuftom and
ufage of the College; and no man had experienced it in a more eminent degree than Dr.
Leland; nor did any man, in my remem-
brance, in the College, ftand in fuch need
R 2   of

of it, tho' his College-debt was not contracted from a neceffity induced by his fituation
in the College, as mine had been. On the
very next day, after I had refufed to ferve
Mr. Hutchinfon with my votes and intereft
on the election, I went, as ufual, to the
Burfar, who then was this Dr. Leland, and
defired him to pay me a quarter's falary, then
due :- he told me he would not pay me, and
that he had *orders* to refufe paying me any
money, till my College-debt was firft dif-
charged : I went to feveral members of the
board, and inquired, whether the board had
given him fuch orders, they all declared that
no fuch matter had been ever mentioned at
the board, and that he had received no orders
whatfoever from the board, except fuch general ones as are given to all Burfars, when
they are elected into the office. This left no
doubt concerning the perfon, who had
given him the orders, for no perfon or
perfons whatfoever, except the Provoft and
board, can give any order to College-
officers refpecting the affairs of the College.
This exertion of revenge and meannefs neither furprifed nor injured me; I had before
been thoroughly acquainted with the principles

ples of the actors in it; and the profits of
my profeffion had about that time emanci-
pated me from the hand of oppreffion in
this particular: I was even in fome fort
pleafed at it; as I knew it would bring more
difgrace on the principal and the tool, than
inconvenience to me: I took no care to
conceal it: and the Provoft, perceiving that
he had injured his intereft, as well as added
a deeper fhade to his character by it, made
fome efforts, weak and contemptible, fuch
only being in his power, to extenuate the
bafenefs of the meafure: in a few months
afterwards he fpoke at the board concerning
the neceffity of diminifhing the debts of the
Fellows: this he did, that he might take an
opportunity of afferting, that I had not been
treated with any peculiar hardfhip: but it is
obfervable, without confidering the circumftances of the precedence, in enforcing the
payment of my debt, with which he honoured me, and the time in which he caufed it
to be exacted, that all fuch fellows as favoured his intereft have, to this day, received the cuftomary indulgence in refpect to
their debts: he has alfo commiffioned his
trufty partifan, Dr. Leland, to declare that

he

he had no orders for refusing to pay me my
salary, except the general orders given to the
Bursar, when he first enters upon his office;
and that such orders, extending to the calling
in of the debts of the Fellows, sufficiently
justified his conduct to me : but here it must
be remarked, that such general orders were
never understood by any Bursar, during the
fourteen years preceding in which I had
been a Fellow, to extend to the stoppage of
my salary ; I had been always considered as
entitled to indulgence, in that respect, from
the reasons I have herein before fully stated,
and to a greater indulgence than any other
Fellow : I had, notwithstanding the peculiar disadvantage I laboured under, lived with
such frugality, that I owed less to the College, than any Fellow who had arrived at my
standing, for a number of years, a very few
excepted ; tho' their incomes had greatly exceeded mine. No Fellow in the College
knew better than Dr. Leland, that such general orders did not extend to the stoppage
of the salary of Fellows, who had no
pupils, for the payment of their College
debts : for he had been a Senior Fellow for
sixteen years preceding ; and, for the greater

part

part of that time, never owed lefs than 1000l.
to the College; often more: his College debt
had been alfo very heavy, when he was a
Junior Fellow: the late Provoft, Dr. Andrews, of benevolent memory, had, through
compaffion, permitted Dr. Leland to remain
thus heavily indebted to the College for fo
long a time, knowing that he had a numerous and expenfive family to fupport, whofe
demands fwallowed up the whole ample income of a Senior Fellowfhip, and that if he
fhould rigoroufly exact the payment of his
College debt, they would be reduced to indi-
gence: thus fuffering the feelings of huma-
nity, in this man's cafe, to filence the calls of
his duty to the College: he had alfo from the
fame compaffionate motives procured for Dr.
Leland the vicarage of Bray, which he has
fince turned to good account. At the time
this man ftopped my falary, he enjoyed the
lucrative place of Burfar, a Senior Fellowfhip, and a church living worth 600l. per
ann. he had been Burfar alfo before; and tho'
he was in poffeffion of an income at that
time of 1400l. per ann. and was for fixteen
years preceding in poffeffion of an annual
income of 800l. one year with another,
about

about eight times greater than my income from the College, yet he would have made grievous complaints, if his falary had been ftopped, even partially, for the payment of his College debt. On the 20th of November, fubfequent to the ftoppage of my falary, this man, notwithftanding all his appointments, returned himfelf in debt to the College, in the fum of 379l. and Dr. Stokes, his friend and companion, tho' prefented above a year ago to a very valuable church living by the College, was permitted to quit the College, in debt to it above 270 l. which is not yet paid ; tho' he too had been a Senior Fellow for upwards of fixteen years. I never was a Senior Fellow, and refigned my Fellowfhip in June 1776, on my election to the employment of royal profeffor of Feudal and Englifh Law, in the Univerfity, and, in the September following, paid off all the debt I owed to the College ; a circumftance of which few, who have refigned their Fellowfhips for a long feries of years paft, can boaft ; and which tends to fhew, what little reafon the Provoft, or his tools, had to ftop my falary for the payment of my College debt, either from its magnitude or infecurity. It cannot
be

be suppofed that this conduct of the Provost
to me gave me an advantageous opinion of
him, or inclined me to pay him any extraordinary attention. I determined to perform
my duty, both to him and the College, according to the prefcriptions of the ftatutes,
without watching for opportunities of ob-
truding any obliging offices upon him. In the
long vacation of the year 1775, the College
cook happened to die, and the Provost, ever
watchful to thruft fome dependant or other
into every employment, by which any thing
is to be gotten, had fixed his eyes on the
cookfhip, for a fellow, one Gaur or Gare,
who ferved him in the capacity of butler : it
was his opinion, as well as that of his patron Blacquiere, that all men were equally
fit for all employments; and that the value
of the office, only, was to be inquired into,
not the duty required, or the capacity to
execute it, of the perfon appointed. I have
already obferved, that this fellow was a
Frenchman or a Swifs, and had been bred a
barber or hair-dreffer. He did not ferve,
even the Provost, in the capacity of cook.
But the employment was worth 200l. per
ann. and tho' he was not capable of performing

ing the duty of a cook, he was capable of receiving the income, and would at any rate make as good a cook, as Mr. Hutchinfon a Provoft. On the death of the cook, feveral candidates, well qualified to fucceed him, applied to me for my intereft as a member of the board : and as it was a matter of fome confequence, both to the Fellows and Scholars, to have a man appointed cook, able to perform the duty, I determined to vote for the perfon amongft the candidates, whom I fhould have reafon to think beft qualified : it was indeed a matter of little confequence to the Provoft, who never dined at commons but once fince his appointment. I had received intelligence, before the board was fummoned for the election of a cook, that the Provoft intended to recommend this Gaur to our choice : I could not think a barber, a land-carriage-officer, and a butler, a proper perfon to be appointed cook ; and I had another objection befides, which had great weight with me : I obferved that when the fervant of a Provoft became a College fervant, he generally turned out infolent, negligent, and fometimes difhoneft: relying on his intereft with the Provoft and his family

for

for impunity. I heard, indeed, that the Provoft had prevailed on a majority of the board to vote for Gaur, but I determined, notwithftanding, to oppofe his election as effectually as I could ; and, every member of the board having, by immemorial cuftom, a right to caufe his diffent from any thing agreed upon by the reft of the board, with his reafons for his diffent, to be inferted in the College regiftry, I prepared a paper, containing my diffent and the reafons for it (a copy of which I have inferted in the notes *) and determined to infift that it fhould be inferted

in

---

* I Patrick Duigenan, L. L. D. one of the junior Fellows of Trinity College, Dublin, and at prefent a member of the board thereof, do hereby declare my diffent from the election of Auguftine Gaur, or Gare, into the place of cook of this College, which my diffent is grounded on the following reafons.

1ft. The faid Gaur is an officer in his Majefty's revenue, ufually called a land-carriage officer, the duty of which office (if he does his duty to his Majefty) will confume fo much of faid Gaur's time, as to render him incapable of attending his duty as cook to this college.

2dly. The duty of the faid office of cook to this College fhould be performed by the man, who is elected cook, in perfon, and not by deputy: it being an office of confiderable truft,

and

in the regiftry, if Gaur fhould be elected. The Provoft fummoned a board to
meet, on the 3d of Auguft, 1775, for the
election of a cook; Gaur was elected by a
majority: I diffented, and prefented my
paper, defiring it might be entered in the
regiftry: the Provoft flew into a violent rage,
and flung the paper at me, in a moft infolent
manner, declaring he would not fuffer it to
be regiftered: I afked whether he was determined to *preclude* me from my right of entering my diffent in the Regiftry, *by his own authority?* this queftion fomewhat alarmed him;
he called to me for the paper, read and examined

and requiring great care and attention, and therefore unfit
to be turned into a fine-cure; and I apprehend the faid
Gaur muft, for the reafon aforefaid, perform the duty thereof
by a deputy.

3dly. I think the election of any private fervant of a provoft of
this College, into fuch a Collegiate office, may be attended
with inconvenience to the domeftick œconomy of this College.

N. B. I had inferted a 4th reafon; which was, that I had
been well informed that Gaur was not bred a cook, but a
barber. However, the Provoft declaring that he was a cook,
I blotted out this reafon at the board, to avoid giving him
offence by a direct contradiction; tho' I gave no credit to
his affertion.

amined it very carefully, and told me, in the course of his obſervations on it, that I had aſſerted a *falſehood:* to this outrage I anſwered, only by bowing, and remarking, that he was thoroughly acquainted both with his ſituation and mine, that he was Provoſt, and I a Fellow. Of this remark, he, at this time, affected to take no notice, but declaring that the paper was an improper one, handed it about to his three partiſans at the board, Drs. Leland, Dabzack and Forſayeth, whom he well knew to be ready to vote, not only, that it was improper, but even treaſonable, if he ſhould give the leaſt hint to them to do ſo. Theſe gentlemen immediately concurred in the impropriety of the paper ; as did another member, I believe, influenced by terror, and to avoid becoming an object of his inſolence ; and then the Provoſt, with great triumph and affected contempt, threw the paper again towards me. Thus did a majority of the board concur, not only in voting away the, heretofore, indubitable right of its own members, but in abetting the arbitrary and ruffianly behaviour of this intruder. Whatever indignation this treatment might have inſpired me with, I had no remedy but

patience

patience and filence : to exprefs my refentment by inftant corporal chaftifement of him,
(the only method of expreffion any way fuit-
ed to his extravagant infolence) would have
fubjected me to immediate expulfion, and I
could not afford to make fo great a facrifice
to my dignity, either as a Fellow of the
College, or a man ; and he was perfectly fenfible of this, or he would not have prefumed
to infult me, no man liftening more atten-
tively to the dictates of moderation, when
fear is her advocate. The altercation ended,
and the board was difmiffed ; but the Provoft's malice and revenge did not end here.;
the aggreffor is always the laft who forgives;
he knew the advantage he had over me at
the board, by the abfence of Dr. Kearney,
and the confequent prefence of Dr. Forfayeth. In about a week after he fummoned
another board, with the avowed defign of
procuring a College-cenfure to be inflicted on
me. I was, at this time, a few miles from
Dublin, at a friend's houfe ; and the Vice-
Provoft, to whom he declared his intention,
with difficulty prevailed on him to adjourn
the board, till he could have an opportunity of fending for me : when I came

to

to town, I was informed, that he intended to accufe me of having challenged
him, and that my remark about his knowledge of our refpective fituations at the
board, when he told me that I had afferted
a falfehood, amounted to one. The extraordinary nature of this complaint, which was
no other than that a man had attempted to
hint that he felt fome uneafinefs, when he
was made the object of the moft brutal
infult, and endeavoured to pique the pride
of the aggreffor, fo as to engage him to de-
fift from treating him with outrage, which
he was neither able to refift nor retaliate,
the time he had taken to prepare his creatures at the board to favour the efforts of his
vengeance, (for he did not complain of the
words when they were uttered, though they
were expreffed before the very fame board)
and above all the vote of the majority of that
board, that my diffent in the cafe of Gaur's
election was improper, alarmed my friends:
they told me that a majority was prepared
to vote me guilty of any crime which the
Provoft fhould think proper to lay to my
charge, and entreated me to make him fome
apology to difarm his wrath. My thoughts

on

on this matter were very different : I knew
the accufation was too ridiculous to be feri-
oufly fupported : I was, indeed, fully fenfible
of the voting abilities of Doctors Leland,
Dabzack, and Forfayeth, and that they were
always at their patron's beck, ready to vote
a molehill a mountain : but I was very certain, that the fourth gentleman, who concurred in voting my diffent improper, would
not be eafily prevailed on to give a vote ef-
fentially prejudicial to one of his brethren,
in a cafe fo ftrongly coloured, as this was,
with abfurdity, oppreffion, and injuftice :
and if this gentleman fhould, contrary to
all probability, difappoint my expectations,
I was refolved to appeal to the vifitors,
and, as the cafe was circumftanced, I had no
doubt of relief : I therefore refufed with
fome warmth to make any apology whatfoever : but the ill-judged zeal of fome of my
friends prevailed on a gentleman, whofe advice to me has always the force of commands,
to interfere, and infift that I fhould make an
apology, and I was at length prevailed on to
fubmit, very reluctantly, and contrary to my
own judgment : I knew, however, the malignant nature and low cunning of the man

I had

to deal with better than my friends, and therefore determined to be ſtrictly on my guard, and to do or ſay nothing which ſhould tend in any manner to injure myſelf. That the words of the apology I was to make might be accurately defined, and that there ſhould be no handle to miſrepreſent them, I wrote down the following form of ſubmiſſi- on, and of this I made two copies; one I gave to the Vice-Provoſt, in whoſe cuſtody it yet remains, the other I kept in my own poſſeſſion : at the time I gave the copy to the Vice-Provoſt, I told him that no advice or perſuaſion of any man on earth ſhould ever induce me to make any addition to this form of apology : and, that the bounds and terms of my ſubmiſſion might be fully known to the Provoſt, before the board aſſembled, that he might be at liberty either to accept or reject it, I requeſted that the Vice-Pro- voſt would carry the copy to him, before that time : the Vice-Provoſt accordingly carried the paper to him, immediately be- fore the board aſſembled, which he read, and declared that he was perfectly contented with it, and that it was fully ſufficient. The form was as follows :

S   " I delivered

" I delivered in a paper to the board,
" which, at the time I delivered it, I did not
" think improper ; but as the board has ad-
" judged it to be improper, I declare, *I fub-*
" *mit to the judgment of the board* ; and as
" the Provoſt *is offended at fome expreſſions,*
" which fell from me, after I had delivered
" in the faid paper, I declare I am very forry,
" for fuch expreſſions, and aſk the Provoſt's
" pardon." The reader will obferve that I
carefully avoided in this paper any admiſſi-
on, either that my written diſſent, on Gaur's
election, was improper, or that any of my
expreſſions had given the Provoſt juſt caufe
of offence. When thefe preliminaries were
fettled, the Provoſt came to the board, and,
contrary to my expectation, and even to the
nature of the agreement made between him
and the Vice-Provoſt on my behalf, began
with every fign of rage and perturbation, a moſt virulent harangue, containing
a long detail of ill-treatment, which he
pretended to have received from me ; and
it confiſted entirely of moſt extravagant
falfehoods, and monſtrous exaggerations of
trivial circumſtances. I was not prepared for this infidious attack. I underſtood
the

the terms of pacification to have been entirely fettled, and that nothing remained
to be performed, but my pronouncing the
apology : I was for fome time in doubt whether I fhould pronounce it or not; but at
length, thinking it the beft way to repeat
it, as I fhould have the opportunity (confidering what had happened) of ftanding on
my defence, with fome advantage, if he
fhould reject it, I arofe ; and, after telling him
that I did not mean to enter into any debate
of the matter, pronounced the apology exactly according to the written form, word by
word, and then fat down. Doctor Dabzack,
(as had been preconcerted between him and
his patron) with an infulting appearance
of compaffion, immediately arofe, and addreffed the Provoft, telling him that the
board would become interceffors for me,
and, after many encomiums on the Provoft's
mercy and kindnefs, entreated him to
pardon me. The Provoft moft gracioufly
condefcended, on the repeated fupplicati-
ons of this *prefumptuous and officious advocate*, at length to declare, that he would
not proceed further in the matter; but
infifted that all thefe tranfactions fhould

be

be regiftered, fo as that a cenfure might appear on record, in the College-books, againft
me; and my orator, who fo kindly and of-
ficioufly interceded for me, being Regifter,
immediately proceeded to draw up an account of the tranfaction, to be fairly copied
into the regiftry. I preferved, during the acting of this farce, a fullen filence. I was agitated by the moft poignant indignation : the recollection is, even yet, painful to me : I found
myfelf at once the dupe of the miftaken indif-
creet zeal and timidity of my friends, and the
perfidy, the low malignant cunning, and chicanery of my enemies, whofe folly was, heretofore, the object of my ridicule : I fuffered
every inconvenience, which could have happened to me, if I had honourably ftood on
my defence, and the board had voted, that
a cenfure fhould be inflicted on me, with the
additional difadvantages of having precluded
myfelf from my remedy, by appeal, and
expofed myfelf to contempt and derifion, by
the meannefs of an apology, which my foul
difdained. But the Provoft was not yet contented ; he was determined to pufh his advantages ftill further: a pernicious cuftom has
long prevailed in the College, of permittting
the

the Regifter to make foul drafts, at the board,
of its acts, fair copies of which he afterwards
inferts in the regiftry. This practice is attended with no danger, when a man of honour and integrity is regifter; but may be,
and is, converted to very bad purpofes, when
the regiftry is in the hands of a perfon of a
different character. Dr. Dabzack read to
the Senior Fellows, who remained, a fhort time
after the Provoft had retired, the account
which he had drawn up, of the tranfaction,
in which it was inferted, " That I had ufed
" *difrefpectful* expreffions to the Provoft." I
objected to this, as the word, which the Provoft himfelf had ordered to be inferted, was
improper, not *difrefpectful*. Dr. Dabzack,
with remarkable agility, went, or rather ran
out of the room, and came back fhortly in
company with the Provoft, who ordered the
word *difrefpectful* to be retained, declaring,
with equal falfehood and impudence, that it
was the word, which he had firft ordered to
be inferted; and, in a few days afterwards,
I was fent for by Dr. Murray, who fhewed
me the fair entry of this tranfaction, in Dr.
Dabzack's hand-writing, in the regiftry of
cenfures. He told me, it had been fent to
him

him by the Provoſt, with directions to ſhew it to me, and inform me, that if I would not agree, that ſuch an entry ſhould remain on the regiſtry, he would cauſe the whole affair to be again canvaſſed before the board: this entry, to my great ſurprize, varied moſt materially, from the foul draft of the account of the tranſaction, drawn by Dr. Dabzack, at the board, contained an account of that affair, entirely different from the facts, and was moſt artfully and wickedly contrived to do me the moſt eſſential injury and injuſtice. I ſhall inſert a copy of it here, marking its variations from the draft prepared at the board, by Italicks. "Dr. Duigenan
" having, at a board held on the 3d day of
" Auguſt, *and alſo on two former occaſions,*
" uſed improper and diſreſpectful expreſſions
" to the Provoſt, the Provoſt was pleaſed to re
" fer the matter to the determination of the
" board : but Dr. Duigenan having this day,
" at the board, *acknowledged his offence*, and
" aſked the Provoſt's pardon, the Provoſt, at
" the interceſſion of the board, was pleaſed
" not to proceed farther againſt Dr. Duigenan
" for the ſaid offence." Before I relate my conduct upon this occaſion, and explain the
villanous

villanous tendency of the interpolations, and the criminality, of the regifter in inferting them, it is neceffary to give fome account of two tranfactions, between the Provoft and me, alluded to in this cenfure. On the diftribution of premiums, by the board, to the authors of poetical compofitions, of which I have before given a circumftantial account, I had refufed to read thefe performances at the board, alleging, as the truth was, that I had not time fufficient allowed me to read them, as they were very voluminous ; one of them, and the moft bulky, a wretched latin poem, of which I read about twenty lines, (probably the purchafed labour of fome indigent Servitor at Oxford) was declared to be the compofition of the Provoft's own fon. When I declined reading thefe poems, or giving my judgment on them, I did not know that his fon was one of the candidates, as they were given in under fictitious names, confequently I could have had no defign whatfoever of depreciating his fon's merit, if any he had, or offending him. Yet, my refufing to read thefe poems, he infifted in his harangue, was a great inftance of difrefpect to him ; as if it was a difrefpect, to one particu-

lar

lar dunce, for a man to refufe to read and
applaud the labours of all his brethren, every
Bavius and Mevius ; for in no other light
could my behaviour, on that occafion, be
accounted difrefpeƈtful to him. The fecond
tranfaƈtion was as follows : there are feveral
Profeffors in the Univerfity of Dublin, in
various branches of literature ; thefe are all
eleƈted by the College, and deliver their preleƈtions and courfes of leƈtures therein : in
his rage of alteration and improvement, he
determined, by his own authority, to compel
all the members of the College, of whatfoever degree, to attend the preleƈtions
of the Profeffors, and iffued his orders to that
effeƈt : it feemed ftrange, that the Fellows
of the College, who are eftablifhed there for
the purpofe of inftruƈting others, fhould be
obliged to an attendance on leƈtures, calculated for the improvement of the ftudents only. He had alfo, in iffuing thefe orders by
his own authority, exceeded the bounds of
his power : for in the 4th chapter of the ftatutes, which treats of the authority of the
Provoft and Senior Fellows, there is the following claufe, " That the Provoft may be
" the better able to perform his duty, we will
" and

" and ordain, that, of the whole number of
" the Fellows, the feven Seniors fhall be, as
" it were, his affeffors, and that he fhall, with
" their advice and affiftance, tranfaɛt all the
" greater affairs of the College, whether
" they regard morals, *learning*, or œconomy,
" and thefe feven fhall be called Senior Fel-
" lows." Such orders then, refpeɛting *learning*, to give them the force of ftatutable obligations, fhould have been iffued by the
Provoft and board : the attendance on thefe
preleɛtions was particularly inconvenient to
me ; I was a *praɛtifing* common-lawyer, as
well as Civilian, and, during term, the duties of my profeffions confumed all my time ;
fuch part of it, as was not taken up in attending the different courts, was expended
in drafting pleadings, and other bufinefs, in
my chamber : I did not imagine that he
would expeɛt my attendance on thefe exercifes ; but in this I was miftaken; for one day
whilft I was fitting in the court of chancery,
he leaned over two benches towards me,
and obferved to me, with a moft infolent air
of authority and rebuke, " That I had not
attended a preleɛtion that day." This infult,
in the prefence and hearing of feveral *barrif-*
ters

ters, from a man too, who was a *practifing* barrifter, as well as I, and fo far my equal in that place, gave me juft offence : my fta-tion, as a Fellow, however, prevented me on this occafion, as well as others, from treating him as he deferved ; and this he well knew : I calmly anfwered, " That I had not attended, and did not conceive my-felf obliged to attend." On this he defired, that I would walk out with him into the hall, with which I readily complied, hoping his rage, which was vifible in his countenance, would plunge him into fome indecency, of which I might take an advantage, this tranf-action happening after he had wantonly and repeatedly infulted me in the College : in the hall he told me, that I was bound by my oath, as a Fellow, to obey his orders, part of that oath obliging the fwearer to obey the Provoft in all things lawful and honeft : I told him, that, in iffuing thefe orders, he had exceeded the bounds of his ftatutable power; that the words, lawful and honeft, in the Fellow's oath, referred to things lawful and honeft by the ftatutes ; that if they were to be taken in any other fenfe, even fo as to extend to things lawful and honeft by the

laws

laws of the land, he might, by virtue of
that claufe of the oath, affume a power, inconfiftent with the ftatutes, and compel
the Fellows to obey him in things not warranted by them, tho' they were prefcribed
as the ftandard and meafure of their obedience : that if he ordered me to do even a
thing of an indifferent nature, which was
neither enjoined nor forbidden by the ftatutes, yet, if I conceived that the performance
of it in any way leffened or demeaned me, I
fhould account it difhoneft, and refufe to
do it, notwithftanding the oath; and that
his iffuing thefe orders, by his own authority, was not ftatutable. His vifage underwent moft violent contorfions, and affumed
a variety of deadly colours, whilft I was
fpeaking ; he quickly perceived, from my
manner, that this was not either the proper
feafon or place, to affume the tyrant and the
bully : to my great difappointment, he haf-
tily turned away, defiring me to attend him
that evening, at nine o'clock, in the College. I went accordingly, and was fhewn
into a room, where I found him, with a witnefs in waiting, as is cuftomary with him.
He had, by this time, perceived, that he had
                                        entered

entered into this difpute with me, on ground not tenable; and, after fome preliminary difcourfe, in which he appeared aukward and difturbed, told me, that he had order-ed me to attend him, for the purpofe of in-forming me, that he did not enjoin attend-ance on prelections, to the Fellows, as a du-ty, but rather requefted their attendance, to add a dignity, and give an appearance of fo-lemnity, to thefe exercifes : I told him, that tho' I never would have attended them on the fcore of duty, unlefs attendance was pre-fcribed by the board, yet that I was willing to oblige him by my attendance on them for the future, whenever I had leifure : confi-dering, that attendance, as my voluntary act, to gratify his wifhes ; and to fhew him the fincerity of this profeffion, I afterwards frequently attended them. This occurrence happened about fix months before his com-plaint againft me, to the board, yet he thought fit to dwell on it in his harangue, as an inftance of difrefpect to him. When I had read the entry, and Dr. Murray had de-livered the Provoft's meffage, I clearly per-ceived, that he and his junto had formed the defign of excluding me from a Senior-Fel-lowfhip lowſhip, as I ſhall preſently explain : this would ſerve two purpoſes ; firſt, it would gratify the Provoſt's revenge, and hold out an example of terror to all the reſt of the Junior Fellows ; ſecondly, I was, at this time, Senior of the Junior Fellows, and therefore firſt in ſucceſſion to a Senior Fellowſhip. His partiſan, Forſayeth, (for whom he had obtained the church-living from government, and who was his moſt active agent, both in this buſineſs and electioneering) was ſecond in ſucceſſion ; my excluſion would place him firſt. The conſpiracy againſt me was evident ; it was alſo clear that the conſpirators, from what they had already done, would not ſtop at any thing to carry their point. After mature deliberation, and conſultation with ſome intelligent friends, it was determined, that I ſhould deliver an evaſive meſſage, concerning the entry, to Doctor Murray, neither expreſſive of my approbation, or diſapprobation ; for as a dangerous crime was already committed, by the inſertion of an entry in the regiſtry, different moſt materially from the one drawn up, and agreed to, at the board, the difference too being evidently

dently calculated to injure, if not ruin me ;
(all which, I had it in my power fully to prove,
and was indeed admitted by the Provoſt, by
his ſending the entry to Doctor Murray for
my inſpection, and cauſing a threatening
meſſage to be delivered to me, with a view
of extorting my approbation of it) it was
the opinion of my friends, and it coincided
with my own, that it was the moſt prudent
method of proceeding, not to alarm the
Provoſt, or his junto, by excepting againſt
the entry, which might put them on their
guard, and ſet them at work to procure a
majority of the board to review and countenance the entry, which I could not be certain that they would not effect ; it being
eaſier to procure a man's approbation of a
thing already done, than of the doing of it ;
and the Provoſt's majority, at the board, de-
pending upon his gaining over one man only,
whoſe conduct was doubtful : three of them
being already avowedly his confederates. If
the Provoſt ſhould reſt contented with my
meſſage, and leave the entry as it was,
without procuring the board to review and
approve it, we concluded that I might at a
viſitation, or at the time when he ſhould at-

tempt

tempt to prevent my fucceffion to a Senior Fellowfhip, lay the crime both of him and the Regifter before the Vifitors, with great advantage, and bring both of them to con- dign ftatutable punifhment: in purfuance of this refolution, I told Doctor Murray that it would not be proper for me, as a fingle Fellow, to exprefs my approbation or difap- probation of the entry, which was there inferted as an act of, or a regiftry of what had happened at, a board, and had been entered there by the proper officer; that if I was afked whether I approved or difap- proved thereof, in my proper place, at a board, and as a member thereof, I would exprefs my fentiments concerning it, but that now I did not conceive myfelf obliged to do fo: and as I therefore would not, in this private man- ner, exprefs either my approbation or difap- probation of this entry, it would be fufficient for him to inform the Provoft, that I did not object to it. Doctor Murray carried this meffage to the Provoft, and the affair fo far ended. To explain the nature and malignity of the interpolations in this entry, I muft re- cite that part of the ftatutes, which regulates the election or co-optation of a Junior into the

place

place of a Senior Fellow. In the 25th chapter is the following clause : " As often as " any person is to be co-opted into the num- " ber of the Senior Fellows, the Provost or " Vice-Provost shall nominate the Senior " amongst the Junior Fellows already elect- " ed, without examination or oath (as being " already performed) and shall demand " the suffrages concerning him, whether " he seems worthy to succeed into the place " of the departing Senior Fellow : *And if* " *such Fellow shall have been convicted be-* " *fore the Provost, and the major, or, at least,* " *any equal part of the Senior Fellows, of* " *an crime, by which he is rendered unwor-* " *thy*, let the next Senior be put in nomi- " nation in the same manner, and so on, " until they shall have agreed upon some " worthy Fellow." Now, with respect to the entry before-mentioned, it is to be ob- served, that the definition of the crime im- puted to me, by the Provost, as settled in the presence of the board, to be inserted in the registry, was the using improper expressi- ons to the Provost, until the ingenious ma- lice of Doctor Dabzack, to give it an higher colouring, procured the word disrespectful

to

to be added, in thus outstripping the rancour, or, at least, the cunning of his principal: the interpolation of the words, " *on two former occasions*," was resolved on in a council held subsequent to the board, with a view of swelling the offence, of which I was accused, into a crime of some magnitude; but as I had not at all confessed, or admitted myself to be guilty of any crime, as may be seen by my apology, and as no proofs had been adduced in support of the accusation, and as the opinion of the Fellows had not been asked, the Provost having accepted the apology, it could not be asserted that I had been convicted before the Provost and major, or equal part of the Senior Fellows; and the council perceived that the crime, of which the Provost had accused me, could not be made use of to prevent my *co-optation* into a Senior-Fellowship, because it was necessary that I should have been convicted of a crime before the Provost, and major, or equal part of the Senior Fellows, statutably to bar my right of co-optation. To rid themselves then of this obstacle to their design, they boldly resolved to insert the words, " *acknowledged his offence*" in the entry, that

T   it

it might appear I was convicted on my own confeſſion : this was a moſt daring interpolation, and of a moſt flagitious nature ; it was no leſs than an attempt to deprive me of £6000, the value of the difference of the income, between a Senior and a Junior Fellowſhip, eſtimating it at ten years purchaſe, for my life : the obtruſion of Mr. Hutchinſon into the place of Provoſt had already deſpoiled me of £1000, as I have before ſhewn ; I was therefore to be further plundered, and becauſe I had little, even that which I had was to be taken from me. The Provoſt, however, conſcious of his guilt, was afraid that this matter might be, ſome day or other, brought to light, and examined into : and to obviate any ill effects from it, to himſelf or his aſſociates, he ſent the entry to Dr. Murray, with the directions before-mentioned : but as murderers are often diſcovered by the very means which they uſe to conceal their guilt, ſo it has happened with the Provoſt, in this affair, for I evaded, in the manner before-mentioned, the expreſſing my opinion of the entry ; and his ſending it to Dr. Murray for my inſpection, with the meſſage before-mentioned,

mentioned, added to my precaution in writing down the words of my apology, fending
the copy to him, by the Vice-provoft, before
I pronounced it, and fuffering that copy yet
to remain in the Vice-provoft's poffeffion,
with other circumftances, enable me clearly
to prove thefe interpolations to have been
inferted without the concurrence of the
board, and their malicious tendency : and I
fhall not fail, if God preferves my life, to
bring him and Dr. Dabzack to their trials for
it, before the Vifitors, on the firft triennial
vifitation, altho' I am no longer a member
of the College. I cannot give my readers a
clearer idea of the deftructive tendency of
this fatal promotion, of Mr. Hutchinfon,
than by fhewing what he has been able to
prevail on Dr. Dabzack to attempt and execute for him. This gentleman had fupported an irreproachable character, before, Mr.
Hutchinfon's appointment ; he and I had
been, for above twenty years, on a good
footing of intimacy, and fome offices of
friendfhip had been interchanged between
us ; I never had given him the leaft offence :
what a lamentable alteration has the Provoft
effected in him ! the procuring a difpenfa-

tion

tion, in the point of matrimony, is the only publick favour he has received from him; perhaps indeed he may have the promife of a government living: yet fuch favours will be but weak juftifications for his joining in the worrying and oppreffing of his brethren: how he may reconcile fuch actions to his own confcience, I know not ; but, fince he has embarked in fuch deftructive defigns, it becomes a part of my fubject, to expofe, to the publick eye, the guilt, nature and tendency of them, to obviate, if poffible, their effects, however irkfome, in refpect to him, the tafk may be to me. I muft clofe the account of this tranfaction, with the following remarks. Dr. Dabzack being Regifter at the time of the commiffion of this crime, he had taken a folemn oath, on his knees, in the College-chapel, with his hands on the Gofpels, faithfully to execute the duties of that office. He had alfo, with the fame folemnity, fworn to obferve the ftatutes, and, in the 11th chapter of them, there is the following claufe : " We alfo command and or-" dain, that the Provoft, Fellows, Scholars, " and all others, fhall encourage, cherifh, " and obferve concord, unity, peace, and " mutual charity amongft themfelves,

to

" to the utmoft of their power." The Provoft's imaginary fuccefs, in perfecuting me, only fpurred him on to further acts of oppreffion : on the 17th of Auguft, 1775, a few days after the tranfactions juft mentioned, he fummoned a board, for the purpofes of depriving Meffrs. Berwick and Davoren, two fcholars of the houfe, of their Scholarfhips : their real crimes were, that they would not promife him their votes on the enfuing election. I have already ftated their cafes fully. After this bufinefs was difpofed of, I afked leave to go to the country: he turned to me in a rage (as I had been one of the three members of the board, who refufed to concur in his defigns againft thefe gentlemen) and told me it was no proper feafon for afking leave of abfence during the fitting of the board. This was a moft abfurd and groundlefs objection : however I replied, that as he himfelf was generally refident at Palmerftown, three miles from Dublin, I had not any other opportunity of applying to him for leave; that I had received retaining fees to attend, in my profeffion, in a town, on the north-weft circuit, forty miles from Dublin, the affizes of which were to

commence

commence on the Monday following, and, this being Thurfday, that I was under the neceffity of then applying to him : he told me, that I had abfented myfelf from the College, for feveral nights in the preceding week, and that he would proceed ftatutably againft me, for fo doing : then, rifing up, defired me to follow him into another room, apart from the board. This conduct furprifed fuch of the board, as were not of his cabinet-council, as much as it did me : no Fellow, fince the foundation of the College, to that day, had ever been queftioned on fuch an account; and it was well known, that feveral of the Fellows were then actually married, and were always abfent from the College at night, particularly his two prime counfellors, Drs. Leland and Dabzack, who were then prefent, and for whom he had not, at that time, procured difpenfations; the feafon too, in which he thought fit to commence this inquiry, concerning my fleeping out of the College, at night, made his conduct the more remarkable, for it was in the middle of the long vacation, at which feafon, leifure from bufinefs, and the purfuit of health and pleafure, ufually induce many of the Fellows, who

who remain in the College (which, as I before observed, is situated in the midst of a
great city) to indulge themselves in riding
into the country, and sometimes sleeping
there. I followed him into this room, where
he directly asked me, whether I had not
slept out of the College, four nights in the
preceding week? I told him, that tho' I did
not think sleeping out of the College any
statutable crime, yet, as he seemed to think it
was, and had avowed his intention of proceeding statutably against me for it, I could
not answer that question, or any other, the
answer to which might tend to criminate
myself, and that, if he expected to convict
me of any crime, it must be by evidence.
He then called in the head-porter, and asked him, whether I had lain out of the College four nights in the preceding week? he
answered in the affirmative. I demanded of
him how he could take upon him to prove
that I had lain out of the College? he said
he could not prove it, but that he received
his information from the porter who kept the
books at the College-gate. I desired that he
might be sent for ; but the Provost, observ-
ing that I was resolved to pry into some
                              circumstances,

circumftances, which he was defirous of
concealing, from the unufual bafenefs of
them (but which, however, I afterwards difcovered, as I fhall prefently mention) and
being defirous of giving fome inftructions to
the porter who kept the books, before I
fhould have an opportunity of crofs-examin-
ing him, refufed to fend for him, telling me,
that he would take another opportunity of
examining this matter, and that I might go
to the country at the time I defired : this
happened on Thurfday, about noon ; I ftaid
in the College, till about the fame time, on
the Saturday following, and he did not think
fit to proceed further in his inquiry ;   I then
went to the country : on my return to the
College, in September, I found a fine of ten
fhillings impofed upon me in the buttery-
books, in confequence of the following entry in the book, in which pecuniary punifhments are regiftered by the College-butler,
which entry the butler was ordered to make
by a note fent to him by the Provoft, and
the entry was an exact copy of the note,
the butler fhewing me the original, in the
Provoft's hand-writing. He fent it to the
Butler, on the Monday or Tuefday after I
had gone to the country.

" Doctor

" Doctor Duigenan, ten fhillings, by the
" Provoft, *for lying out of the College*, on
" the nights of Friday 11th, Saturday 12th,
" Sunday 13th, Monday 14th, Tuefday
" 15th, Wednefday 16th of Auguft, after
" the Provoft had cautioned him not to lie
" out without his leave."

It is neceffary to obferve, that all the
Fellows are affembled at the clofe of each
week, and that all the fines, inferted in the
buttery-books, during that week, are read
over by the Provoft, or, in his abfence, by the
Vice-provoft ; if a Fellow is fined, of which
the inftances are extremely rare, he has then
an opportunity of making his defence, and
the fine is either confirmed or ftruck off;
every tutor, at the fame time, makes fuch
excufes for his pupils, who are fined, as he
thinks proper : that every perfon may have
due notice of what fines are impofed on them,
and the crimes objected againft them, the
Junior Dean, on the evening preceding this
affembly, fits in the publick hall, with the
buttery books before him, open for the infpection of every body, and there inferts fuch
fines in them, as he think fit, for breaches

of

of difcipline ; and the fcholars have an opportunity of urging their feveral excufes ;
which, if rejected by the Dean, may be afterwards infifted upon by their tutors, in
their behalf, at the fubfequent general affembly of the Fellows. The Buttery-books
are alfo open for infpection, at the buttery-
hatch, in the morning previous to the affembly. Hence, unlefs great fraud is ufed
on the part of the impofer of the fines, or
great neglect on the part of the perfon fined,
every member, on whom a fine is impofed,
muft have an opportunity of offering his excufe : it is alfo fometimes cuftomary, with
refpect to pecuniary punifhments on particular occafions, where a man has been precluded by any accident from pleading his excufe, to allow him to do fo on the laft week
of the quarter, previous to the making up
of the quarter's accounts. The Provoft and
Regifter, Dr. Dabzack; both of whom lay
out of the College every night themfelves
with their wives, the Provoft in Palmerftown, and the Doctor *in the city*, contrary to
the very letter and intent of the ftatute, had
conceived the defign of making this accufation of the Provoft appear a regiftered crime
againft

againft me, as if accufation and conviction
had been the fame thing, to aid their original fcheme of precluding me from fucceeding
to a Senior Fellowfhip, and to lay a foundation for expelling me in the end; and the
firft ardour of their malice not allowing them
time to confider the matter fufficiently, they
inferted the crime and punifhment in the
book of cenfures, adding, by way of aggravation, the words, "*after the Provoft had
cautioned him not to lie out without his leave.*"
which was a moft audacious falfe-hood,
the Provoft never having given me any
fuch caution ; but, on the contrary, he had
given the porters at the gate orders to watch
me narrowly, and to keep an exact account
of my going out and returning, with the
ftricteft injunction to preferve his orders fecret from me.   When they reflected a little
that I had not been convicted of, nor confeffed this crime, they determined to proceed with more caution : and, therefore, the
entry in the regiftry was obliterated, and
the note I mentioned fent to the butler; yet
the Provoft took care not to fend this note
either on Thurfday, Friday, or Saturday,
when he knew I was in the College, and
                                        ready

ready to make my defence, but poftponed
it until he was certain that I had fet out on
my circuit, in the courfe of my profeffion :
well knowing that the fine would be confirmed at the next general affembly of the
Fellows, in the clofe of the fubfequent week,
as I would not be prefent to make my defence : and that therefore the crime and
punifhment would remain records, and he
would obtain judgment againft me, as it were,
by default. After he had performed this
job, he went off from the College to a part
of the country, near one hundred miles from
Dublin. When I returned to the College, a
few days before the clofe of the quarter, I
went to the Vice-Provoft, and requefted that
he would permit me to plead my defence
againft the fine, that it might not be irre-
vocably confirmed, and charged to me in my
quarter's account ; but he told me that he
could not venture to meddle with it, and
that it muft lie on the books until the return of the Provoft. He did not return until after the quarter's accounts were made
up, and I had been charged with, and paid
the money, and both crime and fine remain
at this day on record againft me in the
College

College books.   Exclufive of the malignant
art, and low-cunning, he made ufe of in
this affair, to avoid his being under the neceffity of producing proof againft me, and
to preclude even the poffibility of defence on
my part, the punifhment could in no fort be
juftified or fupported by the ftatutes.   The
two claufes of that code, under colour of
which the Provoft claimed the power of inflicting a pecuniary punifhment on the Fel--
lows, for lying out of the College at night,
are the following: the firft to be found in
the 11th, the fecond in the 23d chapter.

   1ft claufe. " Nor fhall any one of the Fel-
" lows, Scholars, and Students, of whatfoe-
" ver rank or degree he may be, remain *in*
" *the city* during the night, nor in another's
" chamber, unlefs he fhall have obtained leave
" fo to do, from the Provoft, or, in his ab-
" fence, from the Vice-Provoft: he who
" fhall tranfgrefs, in thefe particulars, fhall for
" the firft time be deprived of his commons
" during one week; for the fecond, during
" fifteen days; for the third, during a
" month; for the fourth he fhall be *expelled*
                       " by

" by the Provoſt, and the major part of the
" Senior Fellows.

2d Clauſe. " Becauſe it is found by expe-
" 'rience that the puniſhment, by which ordi-
" nary commons are ſubtracted for a time
" *from the Students*, is but of feeble efficacy,
" in reſpect to the correction and diſcipline
" of *ſome Students*, we ordain, that as often
" as the ſtatutes ſpeak concerning the ſub-
" traction of ordinary commons, it may be
" lawful for the Provoſt, or, in his abſence,
" for the Vice-Provoſt, either to impoſe
" that puniſhment on the tranſgreſſor, or to
" change it into another, at his own diſcre-
" tion, which ſhall appear to him to be more
" efficacious for the prevention of tranſgreſ-
" ſions, and for reformation."..

When theſe ſtatutes were framed, in the
reign of King Charles the Firſt, the College
was near half a mile diſtant from the city of
Dublin, tho' now, from the increaſe of the city,
encloſed within it : the ſtatute, which forbad
nightly excurſions from the College into the
city, was deſigned to prevent diſſipation and
vice, the uſual inhabitants of cities : it did not
forbid

forbid nightly abfences from the College, *unlefs the abfentees paffed their time in the city :* the paffing a night in the city is the only crime punifhable by the ftatutes : the vices of a city were alone guarded againft. For the truth and propriety of this conftruc- tion of the claufe in the 11th chapter, juft now quoted, (which agrees with the letter, and the claufe I muft obferve too is a penal one, and to be conftrued ftrictly) I appeal to the underftanding of every man who reads it. The defign and meaning of it is obvious: if the framer of the ftatutes had defigned that abfence from the College at nights, in general, fhould be punifhable, he would have expreffed it, becaufe, from the then fituation of the College, a nocturnal ab- fentee might, with more probability, be fup- pofed to fleep in the country, than the city. Hence it is clear, that if my lying out of the College at night had been proved, yet I was not fubject to punifhment by this claufe, unlefs it had been alfo proved that I had lain in the city ; at leaft a proof on my part, that I had lain in the country, fhould have ex- empted me from punifhment : but, it is evident, from the very words of the Provoft's

note

note to the butler, that he did not, or was not willing to, underftand this claufe; for in that note he ftates my crime to be, lying *out of the College* (not in the city) for five nights. Suppofing, however, that I had been guilty of lying in the city at night, which was not the cafe, and that my guilt had been proved, yet he had no right to commute the ftatutable punifhment of the fubtraction of a week's commons, into a pe-cuniary one, in the cafe of a Fellow, by the claufe in the 23d chapter, which I have quoted; for his power of commutation by that claufe extends only over the Students, and the very reafon given in the claufe for invefting him with that power, if I had been a Student, could not have fubjected me to the power : for it is given to him, becaufe it had been found by experience, that punifh-ment by fubtraction of commons was not always fufficiently efficacious to reform and correct fome Students; but no difcoveries of that nature had been ever extracted from any experiments made upon me; for during my long refidence in the College, I never had experienced any fort of academick punifh-ment, until the promotion of Mr. Hutchin-fon.

fon. He may endeavour to juftify his conduct in inflicting this pecuniary punifhment
on me, by afferting, that, as I was *non-co'd*
(a technical Collegiate expreffion, fignifying
that a man is paid in money the value of his
commons, and does not take them in kind
in the Hall) he could not fubtract the week's
commons, according to the ftatute : but it is
a fufficient anfwer to remark, that if he
could not fubtract the week's commons, he
might have fubtracted their value, whereas
ten fhillings exceeded that value by two at
leaft; fo that he actually proceeded on the
commutation claufe, whofe meaning he as
little underftood, as that of the claufe in the
11th chapter already cited. The dangerous
malignity of the Provoft was in no inftance
fo confpicuous as in this : for as he conftituted the common porters fpies upon my conduct, as thefe porters were all to be nominated by himfelf, from the meaneft and moft fer-
vile of his dependants (their annual falaries being but five pounds each, which, with
their cloaths, and the food they get in the
Hall, is the whole of their emoluments)
and as he pretended, that the fuppofed crime
for which he punifhed me, was the crime

U   -fpecified

fpecified in the laft-mentioned claufe in the 11th chapter of the ftatutes, for the fourth commiffion of which, expulfion is prefcribed as a punifhment, he had evidently projected, and began to execute a fcheme for my expulfion, of which, the record of this punifhment, was the firft of the four fteps or parts ; he imagined he could, with the utmoft eafe; execute the other three; for witneffes againft me would never be wanting amongft the porters, liable to be practifed upon, from their poverty, ignorance and dependance :. even their miftakes might be fatal to my Fellowfhip. I faw the defign, and immediately fet myfelf at work to counteract it. It had been cuftomary, when a Fellow paffed thro the College-gate at night, for one of the porters to attend him from the lodge to his chambers with a lanthorn : I determined to avail myfelf of this cuftom, to correct either the corruption or miftakes of the porters : fhortly after my return to the College, from the country, I bought an account-book, in which I carefully entered the hour, at which I repaired every evening to my chambers, and I caufed the porter who lighted me, to fubfcribe

his

his name to this entry : this was but a feeble fecurity ; but it was the beft in my power. I alfo examined the porters particularly concerning the orders they had received refpecting me. As foon as the Provoft returned from the country, and found the precautions I was taking for my fecurity, from the information of his fpies, he fent orders to the gate, that no porter fhould fubfcribe his name to any entry made by me, or any other paper, in my chamber : the porters afterwards refufed to fubfcribe my entries, and informed me of their orders : thus did he attempt to deprive me of almoft the only certain evidence I could have, of my nightly prefence in the College. But this did not difcourage me : I knew the violence and injuftice of his proceedings would overturn his defign : I ftill perfevered in making regular entries of the times of my return to my chambers every evening : and, that I might have proper evidence of his conduct and defigns, and, for the reafons before-mentioned, having little reliance on the porters, I brought a refpectable * friend along with me to my chambers, one evening : I then fent for the

U 2.   porter

* Dudley Huffey, Efq. a Barrifter.

porter who kept the books at the gate, and examined him before my friend, concerning the orders the Provoſt had given to the porters, relating to me. He informed us, that the Provoſt had given orders, that the porters at the gate ſhould take a particular account of the times of my going out of the College, and returning, and make regular weekly returns of ſuch account to the head-porter, for the Provoſt's uſe; that his orders, in this particular, extended to no other Fellow, but to me; that they were forbidden to ſubſcribe their names to any entry of the time of my return into my chamber; and alſo confeſſed, that they had received directions to keep theſe orders a profound ſecret from me: my friend wrote theſe particulars down, with the name of the porter, that he might be able to give an exact teſtimony of them, on a proper occaſion. To protect his own minions from the effects of any complaints of his partiality on this occaſion, and to furniſh himſelf with a proper excuſe for not puniſhing their nocturnal abſences from the College, were ſome of the reaſons which induced him to procure diſpenſations in the point of marriage, for

the

the Doctors Leland and Dabzack, already
mentioned ; his application for thefe difpenfations being made immediately after his attacking and fining me for lying out of the
College. I fhall here beg the reader to recur
to the Provoft's oath, and confider how conformable his whole behaviour to me, particularly his conduct in this laft inftance, is to
that claufe of his oath, which enjoins him,
" To govern and defend all and every of
" the Fellows, Scholars, Penfioners, Sizers,
" and the reft of the members of the College,
" by the fame laws and ftatutes, without
" refpect, favour, or hatred of, or to, any
" kind, condition, or perfons." And I folemnly declare, that no human confideration, fhall prevent me from bringing him to
juftice, before the Vifitors, on the next triennial vifitation, or fooner, if their graces
will permit me; for this laft inftance of his
tyranny, as well as for his other crimes, firmly perfuaded, that in fo doing, I fhall perform a great fervice to the College, and my
country, acceptable in the fight of the Almighty. This perfecution alarmed my
friends more than it did myfelf. I was determined never to bend under it : it had been
                                    commenced

commenced againſt me, on the moſt unjuſti-
fiable and flagitious motive, to wit, the
Provoſt's reſentment, kindled, in general, by
my ſteady obedience to the dictates of my
duty to the College ; in particular, by my
refuſing, in the firſt place, my approbation
of a Fellow's accepting a Church-living, and
retaining his Fellowſhip, when I thought,
(as I ſtill think, and am ready to prove) that
the acceptance and enjoyment of ſuch a living were incompatible with the enjoyment
of a Fellowſhip ; in the ſecond place, becauſe I refuſed to concur in the election of
the Provoſt's butler (who was, at the ſame
time, a barber and a revenue-officer) into
the place of cook to the College, and diſſent-
ed from his election ; in the third place, becauſe I refuſed to ſupport the Provoſt's intereſt, with my votes on an election of members of parliament, and preferred the ſupport of his Majeſty's attorney-general on that
occaſion. It was carried on with outrage,
violence, injuſtice, and folly : I knew a per-
ſecution, commenced from ſuch a motive,
conducted by ſuch means, would, in the
end, do more injury to the aggreſſor, than to
the object of its fury : I knew by experience,

in

in the cafe of my apology, that fubmiffion
was not my beft defence : I determined to
annoy my adverfary, who perfifted in his attempts to deftroy me, by all the means in my
power ; at the fame time guarding myfelf
from his attacks with the utmoft circum-
fpection, I perfevered in the conduct I had
marked out, with the utmoft patience, con-
ftancy, and activity ; I found him vulnera-
ble in innumerable parts, and I let flip no
opportunity of wounding him : his fubfequent attacks on me, I fruftrated and de-
feated. He had proceeded on a fuppofition
that I was obnoxious to his power in one
particular ; but I found the information of
his fpies, relative to it, groundlefs and illu-
five. At length, perceiving the repeated efforts of his malice to be vain, and ftung
even to madnefs, by fhafts, which his guilt
and folly rendered him unable either to par-
ry or return, he began ardently to wifh,
that he could rid himfelf of me on any terms;
and, the Profefforfhip of Feudal and Englifh
law, in the Univerfity, becoming void by
the untimely and lamented death of my predeceffor, he thought the time of his deliver-
ance was come ; and that I would be glad
to

to accept a place, which would free me from subjection to a man, whom he was confcious I defpifed. But in this he was fomewhat miftaken : he had already exerted upon me all the force of his revenge and malice; and I was experimentally convinced of my fuperiority over him, and that I could maintain my rights and property, notwithftanding all the machinations of him and his junto, nay, that I was more fecure in the poffeffion of them, than he was, in that of his purchafed promotion : the falary of the Profefforfhip amounted only to £360, per ann. that of a Senior-Fellowfhip, to which I was then next in fucceffion, to £700 : to his vexation and aftonifhment, I refufed to accept the place, and confequently to refign my Fellowfhip, unlefs the falary was increafed to £460 per ann. at the fame time declaring that the poffeffion of this place, even with the additional falary, was not an object of my very fanguine wifhes, and that therefore, none of my friends fhould interfere in procuring a grant from the crown, of this additional falary, by which alone, the payment of it out of the College-funds could be fecured. The Provoft, however, effectually exerted himfelf to procure this grant, for
the

the purpose of inducing me to accept the
place, and soon obtained it : I then accepted of the Professorship, and immediately
caused my name to be struck off the College-
books : and I can with truth say, that the
design of writing this treatise, of bringing
Mr. Hutchinson to justice, and of vindica-
ting the cause of learning and religion by an
attempt to rescue the College from impending ruin, was the only motive of my preferring this place, with a salary of £460 per
ann. to the more ample provision of a Senior
Fellowship. To this impartial account of
the Provost's behaviour to me, I shall only
subjoin, before I conclude, two or three in-
stances of his conduct since the general election, to such members as supported the Attorney-General's interest, on that occasion ;
because some of his partisans, who affect
a degree of moderation, have endeavoured to extenuate the guilt of crimes, the
commission of which they could not deny : by asserting that the man's passions
were violently agitated by the opposition he
has met with in the College to his electioneering schemes ; that this agitation has precipitated him into actions and measures,
which

which his cooler reflection would teach him to abhor; and that, when this tempest of electioneering was blown over, his fury, and confequently his oppreffions, would fubfide, and he would become placid and harmlefs, like the ocean in a calm: this is but a weak excufe at beft; but I fhall prove from indifputable facts, that it is not founded on truth; that Mr. Hutchinfon's tyranny is never exerted with fuch force as when he has received no provocation whatfoever for the exercife of it; and that his malice is only whetted by the fubmiffion of the objects of his vengeance. Revenge is his darling paffion, which complaifance and acquiefcenee in the fufferer, inftead of lulling, only roufe to more malignant activity. For, being a ftranger to forgivenefs, he looks on fubmiffion only in the light of an advantage on his fide, to be converted to the ruin of the man, whom he has once confidered as his opponent, even in the moft trivial circumftance; as may be proved by his conduct to me, relative to my apology. The firft inftance I fhall produce as a proof of thefe affertions, is the cafe of Mr. Henry Gamble, Batchelor of Arts: this gentleman is one of the clerks of the

buttery,

buttery, and his place is worth about fifty
pounds per ann. the Provofts for a confiderable time back, had assumed a power of nominating the two clerks of the buttery, not
only without being warranted in the exercife
of fuch power by the ftatutes, but in oppofition to their prefcriptions; the clerks
being College officers, and therefore elective by the Provoft and Senior Fellows,
as may be proved by the 24th chapter of the
ftatutes, De inferioribus Collegii Miniftris.
The Provoft, after the moft preffing folicita-
tions, had, at length, extorted a conditional
promife from Mr. Gamble to vote for his
fon at the election, provided his voting for
his fon did not interfere with the intereft of
the Attorney-General, by menaces of depriving him of his place, unlefs he would
comply with his requeft, *conveyed in an in-
direct manner, but fufficiently intelligible;*
the cuftom of nomination of thefe clerks
in the College by the Provoft inducing Mr.
Gamble to imagine that Mr. Hutchinfon had
it in his power to execute his threat. Mr.
Gamble's inclination led him to fupport the
intereft of the Attorney-General on the election; and before that period, on confulta-
tion

tion with his friends, and examination of the statutes, it was found that Mr. Hutchinson had no power to nominate the clerks of the buttery; and Mr. Gamble's friends agreed, if he had such power, that he could not deprive a man statutably in possession of a Collegiate office, unless he could prove him guilty of some offence, or neglect; the power of nomination not including the power of deprivation: they further agreed, as this conditional promise was extorted from Mr. Gamble by so base and impotent a menace, that he was not only, not obliged, but ought not in honour, to perform it; and that the very promise itself laid no obligation upon him, as his voting for Mr. Hutchinson's son would naturally injure the interest of the Attorney-General, and Mr. Gamble at the election voted singly for the Attorney-General; acting in this particular with more deference and delicacy to Mr. Hutchinson, than the maxims of honour could exact; for, tho' he did not vote for his son, he declined voting against him. In the last long vacation, some months after the election, Mr. Gamble went to the Provost to desire leave of absence in the usual manner: the Pro-

vost

voſt had no excuſe for refuſing him, he therefore complied with his requiſition; but, as Mr. Gamble was leaving the room, he coolly told him, that he was no longer a clerk of the buttery: Mr. Gamble bowed and re-tired. He immediately afterwards came to my chambers, and told me the Provoſt's conduct to him. I adviſed him to appeal to the Viſitors, but the Primate being then at Armagh, and the time of his return to Dub-lin uncertain; and, as the Provoſt had relied much upon the length of time which had lapſed between Mr. Berwick's deprivation and appeal, I thought it neceſſary that Mr. Gamble ſhould give him inſtant notice, that he deſigned to appeal, as ſoon as the Pri-mate returned: I therefore drew up a writ-ing for him, proteſting againſt this deprivati-on as invalid and unſtatutable, becauſe it was founded on the Provoſt's ſole power without the concurrence of the board; and attempt-ed without cauſe, no crime or neglect, hav-ing been proved or even alledged againſt Mr. Gamble: with this paper I ſent him imme-diately to the Provoſt; but, not finding him at home, he ſerved his ſervant with a copy of it in the preſence of a proper witneſs. The

Provoſt,

Provoft, on the next day, being Sunday, caufed the burfar to write a letter to Mr. Gamble, who had gone about fourteen miles from Dublin, informing him that he was reftored to his office: he had confulted with his junto, found his behaviour could not be fupported; he dreaded another appeal, and determined, if poffible, to ftifle in its infancy the clamour his conduct would probably excite, by the celerity of the reftitution: what made the neceffity he was under of reftoring Mr. Gamble the more galling to him, was, that he had immediately after his declaration to Mr. Gamble, that he was no longer clerk, nominated one of the bafeft of his own partifans to the place. Another inftance of his revenge and infolence fince the election, is his behaviour to the Rev. Mr. Fitzgerald, a Junior Fellow of long ftanding, and a clergyman of irreproachable character: this gentleman had been warmly attached to the Attorney-General's intereft in the College, and, being a married man, was one of thofe Fellows whom he had refcued from the fpecial tyranny, which the Provoft defigned to exercife over the remaining married Fellows, after
he

he had fecured his own minions by difpenfations in that particular.   About the middle of the laft long vacation, Mrs. Fitzgerald had contracted a dangerous diforder after her lying-in : the phyficians told her
that nothing would contribute fo much to
reftore her health, as breathing for fome
time her native air ; and fhe had been born
about 100 miles from Dublin : her weak
and critical condition, and the poor accommodations for travellers on the road, rendered fo long a journey extremely perilous ; her
hufband was refolved not to truft her to the
care of any body but himfelf on the road ;
and fhe was as unwilling to agree to any fe-
paration from him in her then doubtful fituation : in thefe circumftances he determined
to apply for leave of abfence from the College.   The Provoft was at this time refident
at his houfe in Palmerftown ; and, tho' the
ftatutes in the 22d chapter, as I before obferved, have prefcribed that the regiftry in
which, members who obtain leave of abfence from the College, are obliged to infert
their names, fhall be kept by the Provoft,
or in his abfence by the Vice-Provoft, yet
Mr. Hutchinfon, to increafe his own importance,

tance, by making himfelf the object of all application and attention, had unftatutably prefumed to abfent himfelf from the College, and indulge in the pleafures of his country-refidence, without leaving this regiftry in the Vice-Provoft's poffeffion, tho' the College was not honoured by his prefence above once in a week: it is true no ftatutable obligation lay upon any member, to follow him into the country, to obtain leave of abfence; nor had he any ftatutable power, when out of the College-gates, to grant it; that power in his abfence being ftatutably vefted in the Vice-Provoft, who ought to have granted leave in the Provoft's abfence, and prepared a regiftry for the entry of the names of fuch perfons as he might think proper to indulge in this particular. No commands of the Provoft to the contrary, or his omiffion of lodging the regiftry of abfentees in the Vice-Provoft's hands, during his own abfence from the College, in any degree fufpending or fuperfeding the authority which devolved on the Vice-Provoft, in fuch a cafe, by the ftatutes. Notwithftanding this, Mr. Fitzgerald, to avoid any imputation on him of want of refpect and attention to the Provoft,

thought

thought proper to go down to Palmerstown, and request leave of absence from him: when he came there, he represented the desperate state of his wife, and the necessity he was under of accompanying her to the country. The Provost, after mentioning that there were but few Fellows in the College, and hinting as many obstacles to Mr. Fitzgerald's journey as he could invent, at length asked him, at what time he would be ready to set out. Mr. Fitzgerald informed him that he should be ready in about four days from thence, and that his preparations for his journey would take up that time, because he had deferred making any, or writing to his wife's father to send his carriage to meet him on the road, until he had first obtained leave of absence from him: the Provost then complied with his request, telling him that the registry of absentees was at his house in the College, and that he would give directions to his servant to leave it out, that Mr. Fitzgerald might have an opportunity of inserting his name and the day of his departure therein. Mr. Fitzgerald returned to the College, hired a chaise, wrote for his father-in-law's carriage, and

X   made

made every neceffary preparation for his journey; then went to the Provoft's houfe, to enter his name in the regiftry, where the fervant told him, he had received no orders concerning him, but that he would apply to his mafter for directions: late at night; of the day, on which he went to the Provoft's houfe, the head-porter came to him, and fhewed him a note he had juft received from the Provoft, containing orders for Mr. Fitzgerald's attendance at Palmerftown: the note was directed to the head-porter, for this *great man* did not condefcend to write to Mr. Fitzgerald. On the next day he went to Palmerftown, and the phyficians having prefcribed daily airing for Mrs. Fitzgerald, he had the misfortune to take her along with him: he left her in the coach, at the Provoft's gate, and went into the houfe, where he was fhewn into a parlour by a fervant, who told him he would inform the Provoft of his arrival. Mr. Fitzgerald waited with the utmoft impatience, full half an hour: his wife's fickly condition, and her fitting in a hackney-coach, the window of which happened to be broken, waiting on a pub-lick road, in a very expofed fituation, juftly

alarmed

alarmed him : he went out to her twice or thrice, to account for his delay ; at length, feeing one of the Provoft's fervants in the hall he requefted him to inform his mafter, that he attended to receive his commands, and had been waiting a confiderable time ; the fervant promifed to comply, retired, but did not return: he addreffed one of his fons, paffing thro' the hall, in the fame manner, and received the fame anfwer : at laft, after waiting a full hour, a fervant came to fhew him up to the Provoft's chamber : when he entered, he found the joiner, before-mentioned, fitting with the Provoft, who immediately, with every mark of fury, infolence and contempt, addreffed Mr. Fitzgerald in the following words, " How dare you, Sir, " have the affurance and prefumption to in- " terrupt me by repeated meffages, when " you were informed that I was bufy ?" Mr. Fitzgerald's aftonifhment and indignation, on this addrefs, may be eafier conceived than expreffed ; but feeing the joiner, and knowing the purpofe of his attendance, (for an affidavit-man was now as well known to be the conftant attendant of the Provoft, as a fetter of a bailiff,) he repreffed the dic-

tates

tates of his refentment, tho' naturally of a
very warm temper, and coolly anfwered,
" That he had not intended to give the Pro-
" voft any offence ; that he had fent no mef-
" fages but two, one by a fervant, and the
" other by his own fon, whom he had met
" with in the hall ; that they were both very
" humble ones, expreffive of his duty to the
" Provoft, and that he had not fent them,
" until he had been kept waiting fo long,
" that he thought the Provoft either had
" not been informed of his coming, or had
" forgotten it :" this apology feemed rather
to irritate than appeafe the Provoft; he grew
more outrageous ; told Mr. Fitzgerald, that
he had prefumed to behave difrefpectfully
to him; that he would let him know there
were ftatutable punifhments to reftrain his
prefumption ; and afked him tauntingly,
whether he was encouraged to treat him
with difrefpect, from the confideration of his
being a Fellow, whilft he himfelf was only
Provoft ? the teftimonial abilities of the
joiner ftill intimidated Mr. Fitzgerald, his
fubmiffion increafed with Mr. Hutchinfon's
infolence ; he told him with humility, that
he had the misfortune to have brought his
wife

wife along with him, for the benefit of the
air, of whose infirm state of health he had
before informed the Provost; that she had
been, ever since, sitting in a very exposed
situation, at his gate, in a crazy hackney-
coach, and that his anxiety about her had
induced him to be more solicitous for a dis-
charge from his attendance, than perhaps
he otherwise would have been. Even this
excuse had no weight with Mr. Hutchinson;
he repeated his menaces of inflicting statutable punishments on him, for his disrespect ;
told him, he was informed that Dr. Leland
would shortly have occasion to go to the
country, and that he would not therefore
grant him leave of absence, as it would cause
a deficiency in the number of Fellows, which
the statutes required the presence of in the
College. In vain did Mr. Fitzgerald plead
the desperate condition of his wife, the Provost's leave of absence, granted to him a few
days before, the preparations for his journey,
made in consequence of that leave, and his
having written to his father-in-law, to send
his carriage to meet him on the road, on a
certain day, which he could not then coun-
termand : all he could obtain was leave of

absence

abfence for a fortnight, which, confidering
the length of the journey, the badnefs of the
road, the poor accommodations for travellers,
and Mrs. Fitzgerald's weaknefs, would be almoft confumed in the going and returning.
This was equal to a denial; and the Provoft
confidered it as fuch; for he jeeringly told
him, that he might hire a lodging in the
fuburbs for his wife. Mr. Fitzgerald acquiefced, and it pleafed God, notwithftanding
this behaviour of the Provoft, to reftore
Mrs. Fitzgerald to her health. Setting afide
the infolence, oppreffion, and cruelty, which
mark this tranfaction, let us fee how far the
partifans of Mr. Hutchinfon can juftify his
refufing Mr. Fitzgerald leave of abfence, by
the ftatutes. I have before given a pretty exa-
act account of the ftatute of abfence, its nature, defign, and the prefent inexpediency of
executing it ftrictly : the reafon he gave, for
refufing Mr. Fitzgerald, was, that, as he
was informed Dr. Leland would, in a fhort
time afterwards, have occafion to go to the
country, he would not give Mr. Fitzgerald
leave to go, becaufe his abfence would caufe
a deficiency in the number of Fellows, whofe
conftant refidence is required by the ftatute,

Now,

Now, in the first place, Mr. Fitzgerald, hav-ing asked leave before Dr. Leland, had a right to be first gratified : no Fellow hav-ing any right, by the statutes, to be pre-ferred before another, in this particular, ex-cept by priority of application : in the se-cond place, the clause of the statute of ab-sence, which defines the number of Fellows, and Scholars, required to be always resident in the College, prescribes, that the Provost shall not permit more than a third part of the Fellows or Scholars to be absent from the College at one time. So that if the sta-tute was exerted in its rigour, two-thirds of the Fellows and Scholars ought always to be resident. But it is plain, that a regard to the due execution of the statute, no way in-fluenced Mr. Hutchinson's conduct to Mr. Fitzgerald; for out of twenty one Fellows, six or seven only were resident in the College; and out of seventy Scholars, not above twen-ty, scarce a third part of either, at the time he refused Mr. Fitzgerald leave of absence : the rest were all absent by his own permission, and Dr. Leland went with him to England, in about a fortnight after, leaving only six Fellows resident. Hence it is obvious, that

he

he chofe to ufe this ftatute as an engine of oppreffion only of the objects of his malice, without confidering the execution of it as any part of his duty. It is further to be re-marked, that there is not, perhaps, one in-ftance, for 100 years immediately preceding the promotion of Mr. Hutchinfon, of any Fellow's being refufed leave of abfence, in the middle of a long vacation. A brief account of his behaviour, on this occafion, has lately ap-peared in one of the publick prints, along with that of other his enormities : this pub-lication increafed the clamour of the nation againft him, and he thought proper to make a tedious harangue to the board, by way of juf-tification, which lafted, as I am told, *de die in diem*, for a confiderable part of three days; and in this fpeech he had the weaknefs to confefs, that having determined to refufe Mr. Fitzgerald leave of abfence, and hearing that he was a perfon of a warm temper, and therefore likely to ufe fome difrefpectful ex-preffions to him, on his difappointment, he had requefted that the joiner, who hap-pened to be at Palmerftown, on Mr. Fitz-gerald's arrival, would remain and be a wit-nefs of what fhould pafs between them : this

this confeffion, coupled with his infolet treatment of Mr. Fitzgerald, without any manner of caufe, fhews he had determined to take advantage of that warmth of temper, which he fuppofed Mr. Fitzgerald to poffefs, by ufing him with unprovoked outrage, and thereby to extort, perhaps, fome unguarded expreffion from him, which he had his wit-nefs ready to record, and which he would not have failed to have made ufe of to his injury, perhaps his expulfion. Some time fince this confeffion, hearing that Mr. Fitz-gerald had declared, he did not know the join-er's perfon fufficiently, to be certain that it was he who was prefent in the Provoft's chamber, during the interview above rela-ted, he has thought fit to commiffion all his dependants, even the joiner himfelf, to af-fert, that he was not the perfon who was prefent, and that he would make an affida-vit to that purpofe. This defence is exactly of a piece with all Mr. Hutchinfon's defen-ces : he takes fome trivial circumftance in an accufation againft him, and if his accufer happens to be miftaken in it, he denies it with great triumph and oftentation, altho' it no ways leffens the guilt of the crime

objected

objected againft him. Now, for a moment, fuppofing that he had been miftaken, when he confeffed to the board, that the joiner was the perfon prefent at the interview between him and Mr. Fitzgerald, how does it leffen the guilt of his behaviour to him? He has not denied that he refufed him leave to go to the country, under the circumftances already mentioned; nor that he heaped the indignities, already ftated, upon him; nor that he kept a perfon in the room to be a witnefs; but he fays, that this perfon was not the joiner; that is, he admits the whole crime objected againft him; but fays, that his affidavit-man, in ordinary, not being in waiting that day, he employed another in his room: it is as effectual a defence, as if an houfe-breaker fhould confefs that he broke open and robbed the houfe, but that he did not break in at the door, but the window. The intermiffion of electioneering *operations* is fo far from abating, that it feems rather to have increafed his infolence: he had the prefumption lately at the board to attack the Rev. Doctor Murray, towards whom he had hitherto preferved fome meafure of civility, not from any re-

gard

gard to decency, but merely from fear of increafing the popular refentment, already violent againft him. This gentleman, for learning, integrity, modefty, and patience, has
no fuperior in the kingdom, and his character is generally revered: the Vice-Chancellor
lately applied to Doctor Murray, as regifter
of the College, and defired him to demand,
in his name, from the board, the copy of
fome entry relative to Berwick's affair : the
Doctor, accordingly, delivered the Primate's
meffage to the board, and Mr. Hutchinfon
had the prefumption to rebuke him with
great afperity, for delivering any meffage
to the board, until he had firft acquainted
him with it ; telling him, he failed in his
duty to his principal, though the Primate's
meffage was directed to the board, and not
to the Provoft, who is but a part of the
board : one of his partifans, Doctor Forfayeth, with equal impudence, prefumed to reflect on his Grace, declaring that he had
made himfelf a party in Mr. Berwick's affair, and ought not to be indulged with any
copies of the proceedings of the board. With
the view alfo of being as troublefome as poffible to fuch of the Fellows, as have refufed,

or

or fhall hereafter refufe, to obey his arbitrary injunctions, he has conftituted the common porters, their menial fervants, fpies over
them ; thefe wretches have orders to watch
the attendance of Doctors and Bachelors of
Divinity, on chapel duties, and to mark
down the number of their attendances in
each week at the chapel, where the fervice
is celebrated in general thrice each day : he
never attends fervice himfelf above once a
week, and very often neglects even that attendance. To avoid the indecency of pro-
claiming the porters to be eftablifhed infor-
mers againft their mafters, the Senior Dean,
Doctor Leland, has notified to the Fellows,
that he is ordered by the Provoft to infpect
into their attendance at chapel; but as he
does not attend above once in a fortnight,
(for all the Provoft's friends have an abfolute indemnity) he can return no account to
the Provoft, but that which he himfelf re-
ceives from the porters.

><88<>88<>88<>88<>83<

Without producing any other inftances
of the Provoft's conduct, I think I have fully demonftrated that he has formed the defign

fign of banifhing from the College all perfons, who poffefs either honefty or learning;
that he has converted all College emoluments
into electioneering *douceurs*; that he perfifts
with unwearied, fuccefsful, and deftructive
activity in the execution of his fchemes; and,
that if he is permitted to proceed in the fame
career for five years longer, (in which time
he will have nominated the whole fet of
Scholars, and fome Fellows, his elections,
as I have before fhewn, being nominations
in effect) the College will be utterly ruined.
The gentlemen, at prefent, members of the
board, who have dared to perform their duty, tired of an ineffectual oppofition, fhock-
ed at a deftruction, which they are not able
to prevent; worried almoft to death by his
petulance, infolence, outrage, haranguing,
&c. and even apprehenfive of daily attacks
on their Fellowfhips, their hard-earned pro-
perties, from his informations, intrigues,
jobs, and chicanery, will embrace, with a
degree of avidity, the firft opportunity of
efcaping from his tyranny, by accepting
church-livings in the gift of the College,
as they become vacant; fo that the board
will be fhortly made up of his own creatures and tools: and what is to be expected
                                    from

from them may appear from the facts I have already stated, relative to them. I hope that every sincere Proteftant, of the church of Ireland, will serioufly confider the effects of fo fhocking an event, as the deftruction of the College of Dublin; I imagine it will require no great perfuafive powers to convince them, that the ruin of the church will be the certain confequence; the glory of the reformation will be laid in duft, and true chriftian purity will yield to the bold, bufy, blind efforts of fuperftition and fanaticifm: for when the only nurfery from whence this church can be fupplied with paftors, guardians, and defenders, is utterly rooted out, the flock will wander without fhepherds, an eafy defencelefs prey to the ravening wolves, already impatient for blood, flaughter, and confufion.

It now only remains that I fhould point out the proper remedies for this diforder, which thus menaces the church with deftruction, and the nation with darknefs, barbarity, and ignorance. The firft and moft effectual remedy I fhall propofe, is a due exertion of the vifitatorial power: I will fhew
from

from the ftatutes the extent of that power,
and its ability to fave the College : in the
27th chapter are the following claufes.
" Laftly, becaufe nothing can be fo efta-
" blifhed and fortified by good laws, but it
" may be eafily eluded, from fome contri-
" vance of fraud, by thofe who are inclined
" to live licentioufly, and let loofe the reins
" of their luxury and luft: therefore we give
" a power to the Vifitors of the College,
" conftituted in our royal charter, *and more-*
" *over befeech them in the Lord,* to repair to
" this College once in every period of three
" years, either in perfon, or by others deput-
" ed to perform that office, and affemble to-
" gether the Provoft, Vice-Provoft, Deans,
" Burfar, Lecturers, Fellows, Scholars, and
" all the Students of the College, and vi-
" fit the College, as well in the head as in
" the members, and diligently inquire of,
" and concerning, all and fingular the mat-
" ters relating to the ftate, advantage, honor,
" and ftatutes of the aforefaid College, and
" the reformation and correction of its *Pro-*
" *voft,* Vice-Provoft, Burfar, Deans, Scho-
" lars, Students, and Servants : to require
" an oath from each of them to fpeak the
" truth in all and fingular the premifes;
" duly

" duly to punifh and reform the crimes, ex-
" ceffes, delinquencies, and neglects, of any
" members of the aforefaid College, how-
" foever committed, which fhall be difco-
" covered in that vifitation, according to the
" quality and exigency of the crimes, ex-
" ceffes, delinquencies, and neglects, and
" according to the tenor of thefe ftatutes ; or
" to take care that they be punifhed and re-
" formed by the Provoft, or thofe whofe
" bufinefs it is fo to do and to do; and exer-
" cife all and fingular the other things which
" are neceffary for, or any way conducive
" to, their correction and reformation, altho'
" it fhould happen that they fhould be ob-
" liged to proceed to the deprivation or re-
" moval of the Provoft, Vice-Provoft, or
" any body elfe, from their adminiftration
" or office, or to the removal of any Fel-
" low, Scholar, or Student from this Col-
" lege (if the ftatutes of the College fhall
" warrant and require fuch removal.) How-
" ever, always provided, according to the te-
" nor of the charter, that nothing fhall
" ever be done either in deprivation, or any
" of the more weighty affairs of the Col-
" lege, without the approbation of the Chan-
" cellor of the Univerfity, (whom we con-
ftitute

" ftitute the chief Vifitor of this College)
" or if any thing be done, that it be held
" void. We alfo will and ordain, that the
" aforefaid Vifitors, befides their ordinary
" and triennial vifitation, fhall have full
" power and authority to repair to the Col-
" lege, and perform all things belonging or
" appertaining to the office of Vifitors, as of-
" ten as they fhall be required fo to do, by
" the Provoft and major part of the Senior
" Fellows, or by the Provoft alone, or by
" all the Seniors, againft the will of the
" Provoft.

" And we charge the confcience of the
" Vifitors, as they will anfwer for it, before
" the Almighty God, and exhort them in
" the bowels of our Lord Jefus Chrift, that
" in doing and performing the premifes,
" they will have God only before their eyes,
" and that, paying no regard to favour, fear,
" hatred, entreaties, bribery, pretences, or
" opportunities, they will diligently attend
" to their office of vifitation, inquifition,
" correction, and reformation, and faith-
" fully perform it in all things, *as they will*
" *anfwer, in this cafe, before God in his laft*
" *judgment.*"

Y

From

From thefe claufes, and the facts ftated
in this treatife, it is evident, that his
Royal Highnefs the Duke of Gloucefter,
Chancellor of the Univerfity, and the
two Archbifhops of Armagh and Dublin,
have it now in their power to refcue the
College out of the hands of this worfe than
Vandalick deftroyer, and prevent its utter
defolation : their vifitatorial power, of compelling the Fellows and Scholars upon oath
to anfwer concerning every thing relating to
the honour or advantage of the College, has
put arms into the hands of their Graces fufficient to repel the hoftile invafion of this illiterate intruder, and vindicate the interefts
of learning and religion : the exalted ftations
of his Royal Highnefs and their Graces, the
guardianfhip of the Church of this kingdom,
committed to the two Archbifhops; confci-
fcience, honour, the very fpirit of the royal
founders, yet breathing in the charter and
ftatutes, and the groans of the fufferers
under this ignominious and baneful tyranny, all call upon his Royal Highnefs and
their Graces for exertion of their authority,
for relief and protection. I, feeble as I
am, have dragged this Cacus from his den,
before

before the bar of the publick. I am ready and able to haul him before the vifitatorial tribunal of their Graces, to be dealt with according to his deferts. Suffer not, great Prince and holy Prelates, this worthlefs intruder, like the molten calf, longer to remain the object of extorted worfhip from the chofen people of the Lord ! pull down this pafte-board Goliath ! who has fo often proudly defied the minifters of religion, the armies of the living God ! the power is in your hands, his crimes call aloud for correction, and the evidence is full, certain, and inconteftible. Tho' I will not fuffer myfelf to entertain a doubt that the royal and venerable Vifitors will liften to the pathetick exhortations of the ftatutes, and to this publick manifeftation of Mr. Hutchinfon's guilt, and apply the remedy in their power for the falvation of this College, Church, and Kingdom ; yet, left from the incertainty of all events in this world, the application of the firft remedy may be delayed or fail of effect, I fhall point out two other remedies, the application of which depends upon the pleafure of the renowned Monarch, who now wields the Britifh fceptre. As the Provoft's crimes give a ftatutable power to
the

the Vifitors of depriving him, fo his incapacity vefts the fame power in his Majefty. The King's patent is voidable by the common law of the land, if it can be made appear, that he was deceived in his grant. In the prefent cafe, his Majefty's confidence has been abufed : Sir John Blacquiere, an obfcure, unprincipled Sub-agent of a great Minifter of the Crown, has for his own emolument procured that Minifter to mifreprefent this College and kingdom to the throne : a man poffeffing no kind of academick learning, except fuch a knowledge of the Greek and Latin languages, as is ufually acquired by a fchool-boy of two years ftanding, is recommended by the Viceroy to his Majefty, as a proper perfon to be appointed Provoft of this College; to be the head of a Seminary, founded for the inftitution of the youth of a whole kingdom in all the fciences, in every branch of ufeful knowledge; and this head too is invefted with a power by the ftatutes, of determining folely upon the literary merits of all the ftudents, of nominating to all the vacant Fellowfhips and ·Scholarfhips, by the ftatutes held forth as the prizes for fuperior learning. In confequence of this recommendation, this man

is

is appointed Provoft, and the extraordinary power of the Crown is exerted to difpenfe with his want of many effential ftatutable qualifications of a Provoft. The deception is glaring and notorious; he has not, however, yet procured a difpenfation to excufe his want of learning; and I flatter myfelf, that if he fhould apply for it, the crown will never grant it. This defect alone is fufficient to avoid his patent: he is a man of obfcure parentage, without friends or connections; he owes all his importance to the effects of blind chance, and the mifplaced favour of the King's minifters here: that favour withdrawn, he will fink into his native infignificance, his original littlenefs! if he fhould refufe to refign an office, the duties of which he is incapable of performing, and his retaining of which is a difgrace to adminiftration, at the defire of the reprefentative of his Majefty here, the proper officer of the crown may be commanded to bring a *Scire Facias* againft him, to avoid his patent, on the ground that his Majefty has been deceived in his grant, and Mr. Hutchinfon's incapacity to perform the duties of the Provoftfhip, can be eafily proved. Another remedy, in his Majefty's power to adminifter,

minifter, is, a temporary alteration of the
ftatutes. I have already obferved, that the
crown has a power of altering the ftatutes of
the College, at pleafure. Let Mr. Hutchinfon (if it is not thought advifable to avoid
his patent) be deprived of all power, authority or revenue in the College, during his life;
let his authority be entirely transferred to the
board of Senior Fellows, and his revenue
be appropriated to defray the expenfe of the
new buildings: all this may be done by a
temporary alteration of the ftatutes, and will
afford effectual relief to the College. His
Majefty's juftice, benevolence, piety, and
paternal regard to his fubjects, will not fuffer me to entertain a doubt, that he will,
when acquainted with the grievances of this
College, extend fuch relief to the members
of it, and to the fuffering church of this
kingdom, as his wifdom may dictate : and
that fuch relief may be fpeedy and effectual,
is the ardent wifh of multitudes of his Majefty's faithful and obedient fubjects, as well
as the author of this treatife.

F I N I S.

www.ingramcontent.com/pod-product-compliance
Lightning Source LLC
Chambersburg PA
CBHW020931030726
47496CB00005B/1135